CLASSIC ALBUM COVERS OF THE 70s

ARTISTE The Nice **TITLE** Elegy **DATE** 1971 **COMPANY** Charisma **PHOTOGRAPHY** Hipgnosis

CLASSIC ALBUM COVERS OF THE 70s

AUBREY POWELL

Paper Tiger

Paper Tiger
An imprint of Dragon's World
Dragon's World Ltd
Limpsfield
Surrey RH8 0DY
Great Britain

First published by Dragon's World Ltd 1994

The catalogue record for this book
is available from the British Library

ISBN 1 85028 155 6

Editor Julie Davis
Designer Paul Cooper
Art Director John Strange
Editorial Director Pippa Rubinstein

Printed in Italy

Contents

Foreword by Richard Evans   6

Introduction   7

1970   10

1971   22

1972   36

1973   52

1974   70

1975   96

1976   116

1977   128

1978   144

1979   160

Afterword   188

Biography   189

Index   190

Foreword

Richard Evans

Richard Evans has been involved in the visual side of the music industry for more than twenty years. He has designed album covers for artists as diverse as Public Image Limited and Robert Plant. His association with The Who, which began in 1976 with a nude photo session with Keith Moon, has continued through to 1994 with the design of the box set The Who: Thirty Years of Maximum R&B. He now lives in Los Angeles.

It would be very easy to say what a peculiar decade the seventies was. If you compare the beginning of the seventies with the end of the decade, how strangely different and poles apart the two, at first, would seem. Think of the political climate. Think of the fashion. Think of the music. Think of Pink Floyd. Then think of The Damned. But think again. Is that not the case with every decade? Wasn't 1961 a million miles away from 1970? Did 1990 bear any resemblance to 1981? By 1970 The Beatles had gone their separate ways and by 1980 so too had The Sex Pistols. Begin and end; begin and end. Was The Who's *Live at Leeds* reborn as The Clash's *London Calling*? Or, wait a minute, weren't the Jam supposed to be The Who? Who emulates who? Syd Barrett? Sid Vicious? What goes round, eh? To every action there's an equal and opposite reaction. Or at least that's what I was taught in school.

To have been an album cover designer in the seventies was to be working in a decade that strutted in dressed like a pompadoured harlot and left, disillusioned, in rags. My own beginnings in album cover design began with Hipgnosis in 1973. Po had asked me to help them with the graphics on the Floyd's *A Nice Pair* album. The gatefold cover was one of those elaborate cosmic designs that Hipgnosis did so well. Visual puns and surreal mystery flowed from every corner. But on the inside we made it look as if the designer had got bored with his neatness and had let things slip. The photographs had rips and tears in them. There was a coffee cup ring on one of the prints and blow me down if the designer hadn't scribbled his date's phone number on the artwork! I remember how difficult it had been to make the artwork look authentically messy. And yet, within four years I was packing my airbrush away for good, bleaching my, now spiky, hair and learning how to vomit on my artwork like the best of them. Anarchy in the UK!

Nevertheless, whether you remember the seventies because of the striking originality of *Dark Side of the Moon* or the campness of David Bowie's *Aladdin Sane* or because of The Sex Pistols' *Never Mind the Bollocks* or Blondie's *Parallel Lines*, the fact remains that those covers perfectly echoed the time, the place, the climate and the circumstance. Compare The Doors' *Morrison Hotel* with Ian Dury's *New Boots and Panties*. Compare *Led Zeppelin III* with PIL's *Metal Box*. Visual similiarities true, but the major connection is that they were all just right for their own time. Every dog really does have his day. But at the end of the day the song remains the same.

I think it was Mick Jones of The Clash who once said, 'I've never listened to a Led Zeppelin album. I don't have to. Just looking at their album covers makes me want to puke.' But wait, hasn't PIL's elaborate *Metal Box* now become as pompous as Led Zeppelin's *Presence*? Watch Out! What you resist, you become.

Now, do I put a cow on my album cover or a flying pig?

Introduction

By and large, the seventies were a mean, gloomy, dark and turbulent decade. America was still involved in its ignoble and ungracious defeat in Vietnam. And if that wasn't bad enough, it was also rocked by the Watergate scandal.

Britain was scarcely a better place. It voted out Prime Minister Wilson's youthful, dreamy, swinging, socialist Utopia in favour of Edward Heath's Conservative misrule, which led to widespread union unrest, power cuts and the enforced three-day working week.

Wilson returned to office in 1974 but, with inflation spiralling out of control, he never recovered the popularity he had enjoyed in the sixties.

And what of the rest of the world in the seventies? The Middle East war of 1973 bequeathed to the West the oil price rises which fuelled inflation everywhere (and for a while threatened the record industry with a world-wide vinyl shortage). Vietnam's trauma was increased by America denying the war-ravaged land economic aid and reparation. Cambodia was decimated by Pol Pot's genocidal policies. West Germany responded to the terrorist rage of the Baader-Meinhof group with computer surveillance of its populace.

The seventies were indeed a gloomy and often vile time.

In a way, the best thing about the seventies was the speed with which it dispatched the hippy dreams of a rock Utopia, of rock music as a binding communal or authentic experience. As the murder at the Rolling Stones' free concert at Altamont in 1969 proved, rock Utopia could no longer deal with or contain the divergent and often conflicting desires straining to express themselves. Popular music very quickly fragmented in the beginning of the decade, resulting in rich, myriad forms of expression, and no end of strange, bastard crossbreeds, each of them illuminating different areas of experience.

In Britain the man who irrevocably cut the seventies' ties with the previous decade was David Bowie. With his flair for self-creating myth, he made the front cover of *Melody Maker* with possibly the single most exciting announcement the music press ever witnessed. Publicly proclaiming his bisexuality, he opened up the pop audience to all manner of gender experiment and sexual play.

Under the shelter of the Glam Rock camp, flamed into being by Bowie's Ziggy Stardust persona, young people could express their sexual preference away from proscriptive public glare. Bowie's coming out undoubtedly furthered gay liberation.

At a stroke, his announcement severed pop from rock's growing denim-clad obsession with Roots and Authenticity. Bowie introduced the freedom and pleasure of self-created personae that could be discarded as soon as they had served their purpose. From his idol, Andy Warhol, he had learnt the related arts of image creation and media manipulation. His LP releases were cleverly co-ordinated campaigns, designed to establish each new Bowie persona in the public mind. After the music, the pivot of the campaign would be the cover artwork.

In the days before the pop video, the record sleeve was the most important shot the artist had at getting across his self-image. In Bowie's case it was all important for his sleeves to introduce the characters he would later bring to life when he toured. Added to that, he fully understood how well they served, both as points of sale, and as pin-ups in teenagers' bedrooms. Whatever his reasoning, Bowie undoubtedly created the most memorable characters of the early to mid-seventies, and the cover art helped fix them – Ziggy Stardust, Aladdin Sane, the Thin White Duke (from *Station To Station*) – in the popular imagination.

In Britain, Bowie was not alone in his glamorization of popular music. The early Roxy Music were arguably even more sophisticated in their fusion of art and pop. They matched their delirious and deliberately artificial electronic treatments of rock – constructed Frankenstein fashion from dead rock 'n' roll riffs, science fiction and B-movie imagery – to cover girl sleeves that projected a past ideal of beauty into the day after tomorrow.

Others were sheltering under the umbrella of Glam, like those brickies in Boots' make-up The Sweet, who took Bowie to trashier and tackier extremes. In the USA the schlock theatrical horror merchant Alice Cooper and the New York Dolls, who came on like heroin-addled hookers mimicking Mick Jagger and Keith Richards, were discovering much the same things.

Not everyone in rock blurred sexualities and genres; indeed, many rock artists, although rooted in the sixties, seemed conservative in comparison with their more outrageous colleagues.

In retrospect, stars of the seventies seemed to be making music against impossible odds. For one, they had the soured sixties' dream of rock Utopia to live down or live up to, and along with this the sense that music would never be that good, clear or innocent again. Even harder, they had to deal with their own exhaustion after the sixties' debilitating adventures in drugs, combined with their phenomenally fast rise to stardom.

Hardest of all, music was no longer the social pivot it had been just a few years earlier. The more rock stars took time out to recover from their excesses in the sixties and prepare themselves for the yet greater debaucheries that their new-found status afforded them, the more isolated they became from the world experienced by their fans.

The communal impulse behind such massive tribal gatherings as the Woodstock festival in the sixties was erased in the seventies by the money-spinning capacity of the sports-stadium rock concerts that marked the music industry's 'coming of age'. New studio technology provided musicians with previously unheard of multitrack facilities, which allowed them to run up massive bills through endless overdubs. Thus art – or progressive – rock was born.

This genre seemed to spring out of an attempt to dignify rock itself with classical and artistic pretensions, and resulted in tricky musical structures laden with berserk baroque keyboard blasts and ornate guitar solos. The sleeves of this time serve as pointers to the depth of their pretensions, with artwork that was frequently fascinating, but completely in a world of its own.

In the case of Yes, artist Roger Dean created a Tolkien-like universe for the group's music to expand into.

However, the more complicated the music, the longer it took to make albums. Extended studio time placed musicians at an even farther remove from reality. And increased costs had to be recouped through higher record sales. Thus the rock industry devised a ruthlessly efficient cycle of recording, record release and stadium tour to maximize the profits. Now rock stars' status was no longer measured in their music, but in the size of the stadiums they filled, and the number of units (that is, records) they shifted.

In order to fill the stadiums, music had to pump itself up in size. It did so either through taking the progressive rock route of over-elaboration or, more acceptably, by simply turning up the volume. The heavy metal pioneered by the likes of Led Zeppelin seemed tailor-made to be played in American stadiums.

Although if their prime concern was the physical impact of brutalized blues riffs played at peak volume to sensation-hungry male teens, Led Zeppelin had, in addition, their own agenda of power and magic to get across. This was accomplished through the runes and other mystic references they spread through their record cover artworks and music, and the eastern motifs they wove through some of the densest and most potent records ever made.

When the Sex Pistols burst like teen-pimple pus on the mirror they held up to 1976 Britain, all the frustration of growing up stunted in a depressed and demoralized state still in thrall to the petty pomp of its imperial past, came to the surface. Punk channelled the era's simmering resentments into great, vile, foaming gobbets of song that indelibly stained the British music industry's aspirations to respectability.

It was also the conduit through which no end of wonderfully warped and twisted figures could leave behind shining slime trails of art despite, and because of, their minimal grasp of music. For music was but one component of punk.

Punk was compounded from music/noise, the crude burping statement, artwork and graffiti. Indeed, punk was defined as much by its designers as its musicians. The newspaper ragouts of rage, the grafted-on situationist slogans, the Dada-defaced images, the faded xerox textures gifted to punk by Jamie Reid and Sex Pistols manager Malcolm McLaren no sooner satirized the cityscapes of Britain, than they became part of it. Timed to coincide with the Queen's Silver Jubilee celebrations of 1977, McLaren cast himself as a latterday Fagin set to loose his gang of pickpocketing punks, primed with fun-anarchist preaching, on the crowds.

But for all its Stalinist intent of establishing 1977 as rock year zero, punk failed, precisely because it could not overcome its own will to survive. It was somehow transformed into the glibly phrased New Wave, represented in Britain by the jokey Stiff label, and in America by the likes of The Cars, whose idea of what it was all about did not seem to extend beyond matching three-minute precision pop to a vacuous Vargas-inspired pin-up cover (*Candy-O*) in a diminished echo of Roxy Music's early seventies sleeves.

And despite McLaren's protestations about punk being his great British invention, its real precursors lay in mid-seventies American music, like the driven electronics of Suicide, the machine rhythms of Chrome, the 'splatterpoesie' of Patti Smith (whose Robert Mapplethorpe-shot Horses artwork is possibly the single most striking sleeve of the period). Unlike the aforementioned Americans, British punk's biggest failure was its inability to seriously destabilize rock music itself.

In terms of nihilism, punk, which was presented as the voice of the working class, was outmanoeuvred by the decade's most pervasive – and often most reviled – music: DISCO.

Here was a music that revelled in its functional anonymity and was universally popular. The best disco was funk monotony diverted through the European dance electronics of Kraftwerk and the Munich-based Giorgio Moroder. Producer orientated, its stars from – Donna Summer through Grace Jones and Sylvester – were stuffed blouses and shirt fronts for the regular insistent beat. Yet out of these unpromising raw materials came trance musics, like Cerrone's 'Love in C Minor' or Donna Summer's 'I Feel Love' which were every bit as engrossing as Michael Nyman and his music for Peter Greenaway's films and *The Piano*.

For all punk's political and satirical clout, it was in the final count little more than a savagely razored form of R'n'B. Its trad roots ultimately limited the accuracy of its diagnoses, both of music and of 1977 Britain. But then punk rejected the rock establishment and anything with pretensions to quality, replacing it with the spontaneous and ultimately disposable.

Record cover design as an 'art form' descended into a mish-mash of torn photos and deliberate coffee stains, and never really recovered. By the time the music business had welcomed and absorbed this last safety-pinned prodigal into its corporate bosom, all trace of the original Art was gone.

Only the packaging remained.

19 70

HONG KONG FLU KILLS 2,850 IN ONE WEEK

16 January. In the highest weekly figure since 1933, the Hong Kong A2 flu virus killed 2,850 people last week. On Christmas and Boxing Day alone 731 died, although despite the overall increase in the total number of deaths, a closer examination of the figures suggests that the epidemic is now past its peak.

BIAFRAN REVOLT CRUSHED

21 January Western journalists who have been able to visit the former territory of Biafra – since the rebels surrendered to the Nigerian federal government – have reported horrific scenes of starvation, looting and rape. The Spanish Princess Cecile de Bourbon-Parma, who escaped from Biafra shortly before the take-over says: 'There was a massacre as the federal troops advanced. All the men were killed, the women were raped and the fate of the children is uncertain.' Lord Hunt, Britain's special envoy, said on his return that people were returning home looking 'in no way undernourished'.

FIRST 'JUMBO' ARRIVES LATE AT HEATHROW

23 January A giant airliner, known as a 'jumbo', landed at Heathrow airport today, three hours behind schedule. The airport's facilities could scarcely cope and much luggage went astray in the crush. There are fears that schedules at the airport may be seriously disrupted by the turbulence caused by the giant jet.

RUSSELL, PASSIONATE THINKER, DIES AT 97

2 February 'Three passions have governed my life: the longing for love, the search for knowledge and the unbearable pity for the sufferings of mankind.' Bertrand Russell, who began his autobiography with these words, died today, aged 97.

BEATLES IN COURT BATTLE

9 April An era is over. The Beatles, erstwhile Fab Four, one time psychedelic pioneers, and most recently squabbling businessmen, have final dissolved the partnership that for many young people was the most influential of the past decade.

NIXON SENDS TROOPS INTO CAMBODIA

30 April President Nixon tonight sent US combat troops to attack Communist bases in Cambodia. This announcement, which is certain to cause bitter controversy, was made in a surprise television address to the nation. 'I would rather be a one-term president than see America become a second-rate power and accept the first defeat in its history', he said.

US DEMONSTRATORS SHOT AT ANTI-WAR PROTEST IN KENT STATE

4 May Four students, two of them girls, were shot dead by National Guard soldiers at Kent State University in Ohio today. The Guard shot into a crowd of anti-war demonstrators, injuring eleven of them, on the third day of violent rioting at this previously non-violent university.

ARTISTE Pink Floyd TITLE Atom Heart Mother DATE 1970 COMPANY Harvest PHOTOGRAPHY Hipgnosis/John Blake

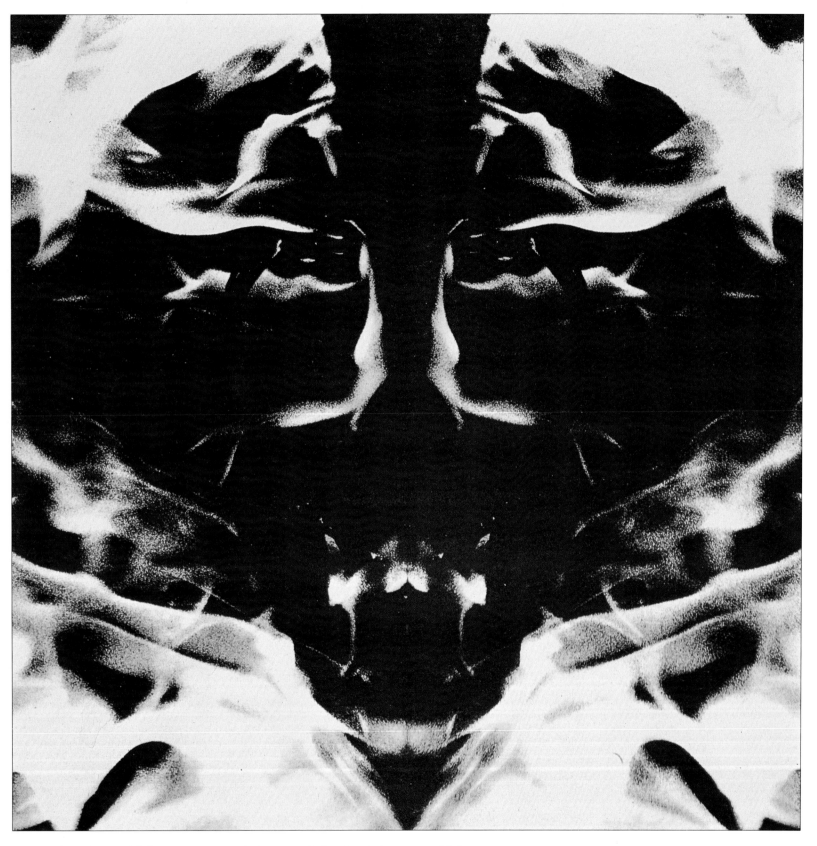

ARTISTE Mott The Hoople TITLE Mad Shadows DATE 1970 COMPANY Island DESIGN Peter Sanders & Ginny Smith PHOTOGRAPHY Gabi Nasemann

ARTISTE The Mothers of Invention TITLE Weasels Ripped My Flesh DATE 1970 COMPANY Bizarre DESIGN Neon Park

ARTISTE Syd Barrett TITLE The Madcap Laughs DATE 1970 COMPANY EMI (Harvest)
DESIGN & PHOTOGRAPHY Hipgnosis

ARTISTE Yes TITLE Time And A Word DATE 1970 COMPANY Atlantic
DESIGN & PHOTOGRAPHY Laurence Sackman DESIGN CO-ORDINATION Graphreaks

ARTISTE The Who TITLE Live At Leeds DATE 1970 COMPANY Polydor (Track) DESIGN Graphreaks

ARTISTE Led Zeppelin TITLE Led Zeppelin III DATE 1970 COMPANY Atlantic DESIGN Zacron

ARTISTE Cochise TITLE Cochise DATE 1970 COMPANY United Artists DESIGN Hipgnosis

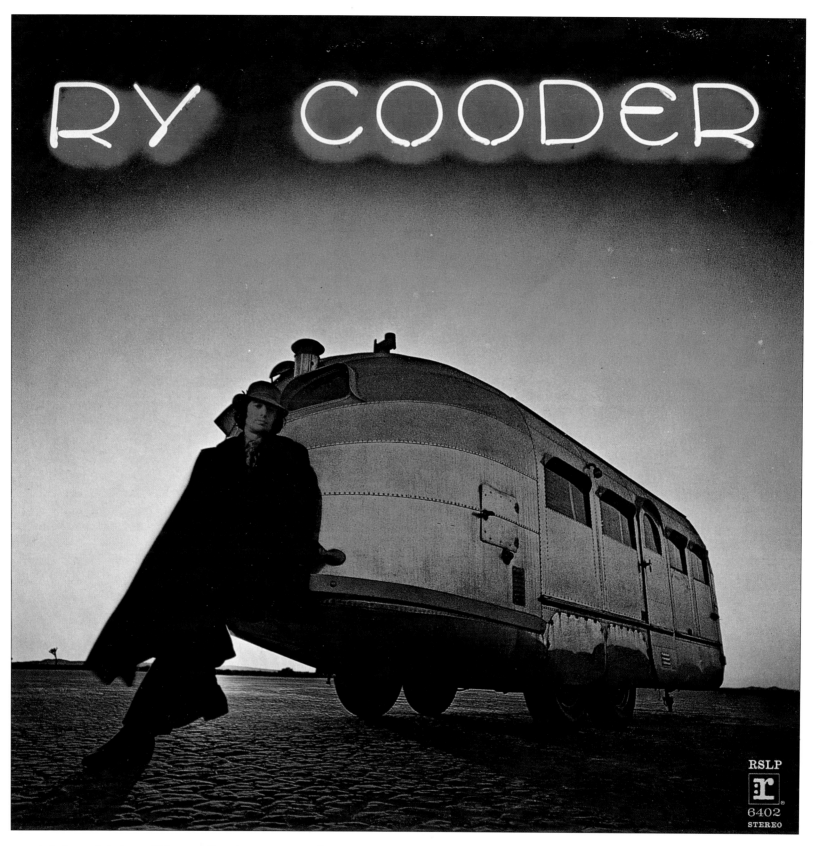

ARTISTE Ry Cooder TITLE Ry Cooder DATE 1970 COMPANY Warner Bros PHOTOGRAPHY Frank Bez

ARTISTE The Byrds **TITLE** Sweetheart of the Rodeo **DATE** 1970 **COMPANY** Columbia **DESIGN** Craig Butler-Synder/Butler Advertising **LINE DRAWINGS** Joe Mora **ART DIRECTION** John Berg

ARTISTE The Doors TITLE Morrison Hotel DATE 1970 COMPANY Elektra/Asylum DESIGN Gary Burden PHOTOGRAPHY Henry Diltz

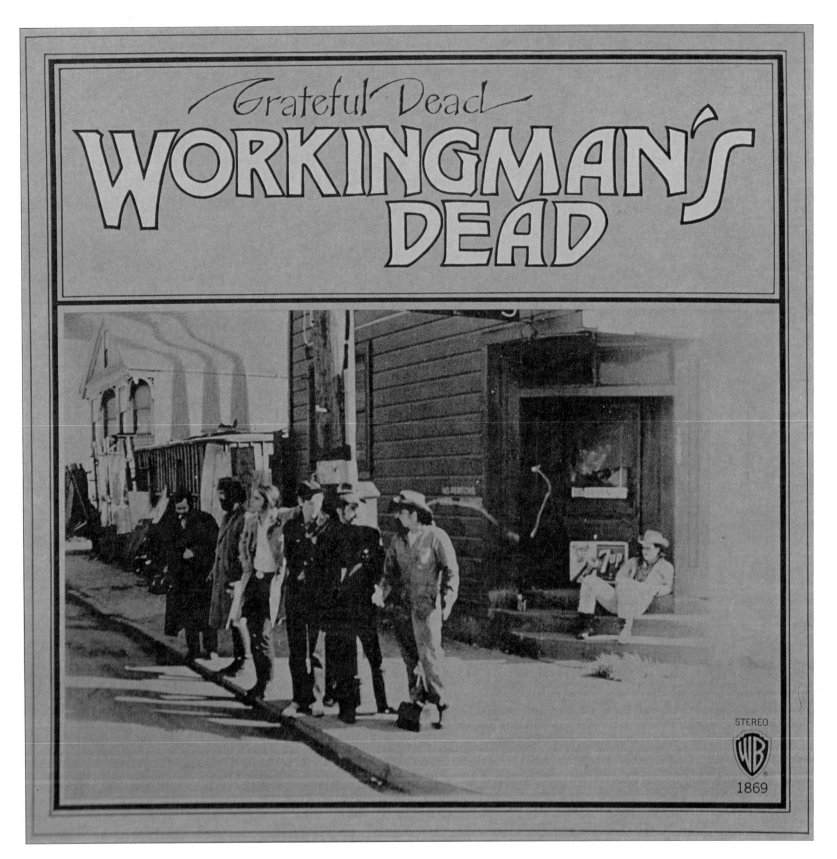

ARTISTE Grateful Dead TITLE Workingman's Dead DATE 1970 COMPANY Warner Bros DESIGN Mouse Studios with Toon n Tee

ARTISTE Miles Davis TITLE Bitches Brew DATE 1970 COMPANY CBS (USA) DESIGN John Berg ILLUSTRATION Abdul Mati Klarwein

SIXTY-SIX DIE AS FOOTBALL BARRIERS COLLAPSE IN GLASGOW

2 January Two hundred football fans were crushed as crowd barriers at Ibrox Park stadium in Glasgow collapsed today. By the time rescuers had forced a path through the mangle of twisted metal poles on the terracing to reach the heap of bodies, they found sixty-six people were dead.

MANSON CONVICTED OF TATE MURDERS

25 January 'You won't outlive this, old man', was murderer Charles Manson's response to the judge when a Los Angeles jury found him and three co-defendants guilty of the murder of the actress Sharon Tate and four others at her Beverley Hills home.

BRITISH CURRENCY GETS A NEW POINT

15 February After centuries of dealing in illogical – yet lovable – pounds, shillings and pence, Britons found themselves battling with decimal currency today. Despite a claim by Lord Fiske, chairman of the Decimal Currency Board, that 'all was going well', many found difficulty in understanding the new system.

ASTRONAUTS GO FOR DRIVE ON MOON

31 July Two astronauts went for a drive on the moon today, picking their way between boulders and craters, and covering several miles in their moon 'rover', with its communications aerial like an inverted parasol. Although their vehicle's front-wheel steering did not work they were able to manoeuvre using the rear wheels.

ROCK STARS RAISE CASH FOR BANGLADESH

1 August Led by former Beatle George Harrison, some of rock's finest artists, including Ravi Shankar, Eric Clapton and Ringo Starr, played and sang for charity tonight, at two sell-out shows in New York's Madison Square Garden. More than 40,000 fans attended the performances, and Harrison hopes to send more than $250,000 to help refugees from Bangladesh.

INDIA DEFEATS PAKISTAN

17 December The two-week war between India and Pakistan ended today in defeat for Pakistan. President Khan swallowed his pride and accepted Mrs Gandhi's ceasefire ultimatum. Pakistan was stunned by his capitulation. Revenge-seeking bands of guerrillas continued to roam the streets last night, despite the Indian commander's call for a bloodless transfer of power.

CHRISTMAS BOMBING CAMPAIGN HITS ULSTER

20 December It looks like a bleak holiday for Northern Ireland as the IRA steps up its bombing campaign of major centres like Belfast and Londonderry, now thronged with shoppers preparing for Christmas.

ARTISTE Rolling Stones TITLE Sticky Fingers DATE 1971 COMPANY Atlantic (Rolling Stones) DESIGN Andy Warhol

ARTISTE Led Zeppelin TITLE Led Zeppelin IV DATE 1971 COMPANY Atlantic
DESIGN 'The Hermit' Barrington Colby/Mom

ARTISTE Traffic TITLE The Low Spark of High Heeled Boys DATE 1971 COMPANY Island
DESIGN Tony Wright PHOTOGRAPHY Richard Polak

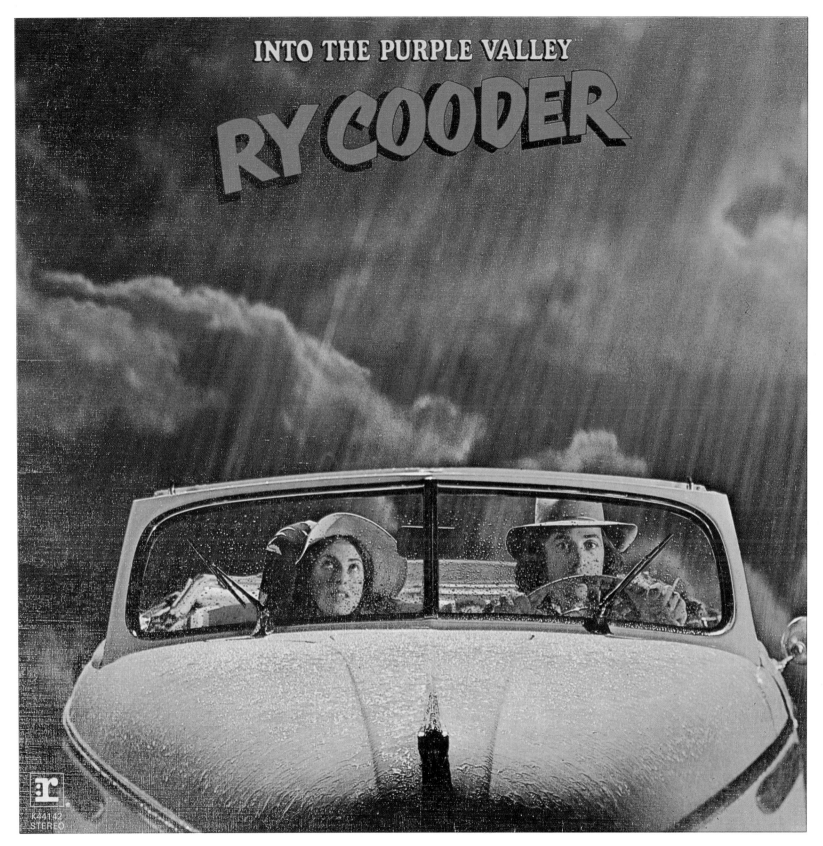

ARTISTE Ry Cooder TITLE Into The Purple Valley DATE 1971 COMPANY Warner Bros (Reprise) DESIGN Mike Salisbury TYPOGRAPHY Dave Bhang

ARTISTE Jefferson Airplane TITLE Bark DATE 1971 COMPANY RCA (Grunt) DESIGN Acy Lehman ILLUSTRATION Grace Slick & B. Thomas (Bag)

ARTISTE Grateful Dead TITLE American Beauty DATE 1971 COMPANY Warner Bros DESIGN Kelly/Mouse Studios

ARTISTE Genesis TITLE Nursery Cryme DATE 1971 COMPANY Charisma DESIGN Paul Whitehead. Inspired by 'Musical Box'

ARTISTE The Nice TITLE Elegy DATE 1971 COMPANY Charisma PHOTOGRAPHY Hipgnosis

ARTISTE Gerry Rafferty TITLE Can I Have My Money Back? DATE 1971 COMPANY Transatlantic DESIGN Patrick

ARTISTE Osibisa TITLE Osibisa DATE 1971 COMPANY MCA (EMI) DESIGN Roger Dean

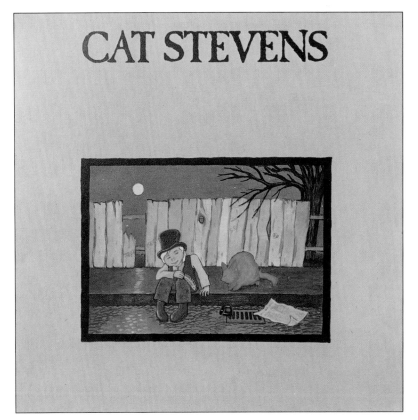

ARTISTE Cat Stevens TITLE Teaser And The Firecat DATE 1971 COMPANY Island PAINTING Cat Stevens

ARTISTE Hawkwind TITLE In Search Of Space DATE 1971 COMPANY United Artists DESIGN Barney Bubbles

ARTISTE Van Der Graaf Generator TITLE Pawn Hearts DATE 1971 COMPANY Charisma DESIGN Keith Morris

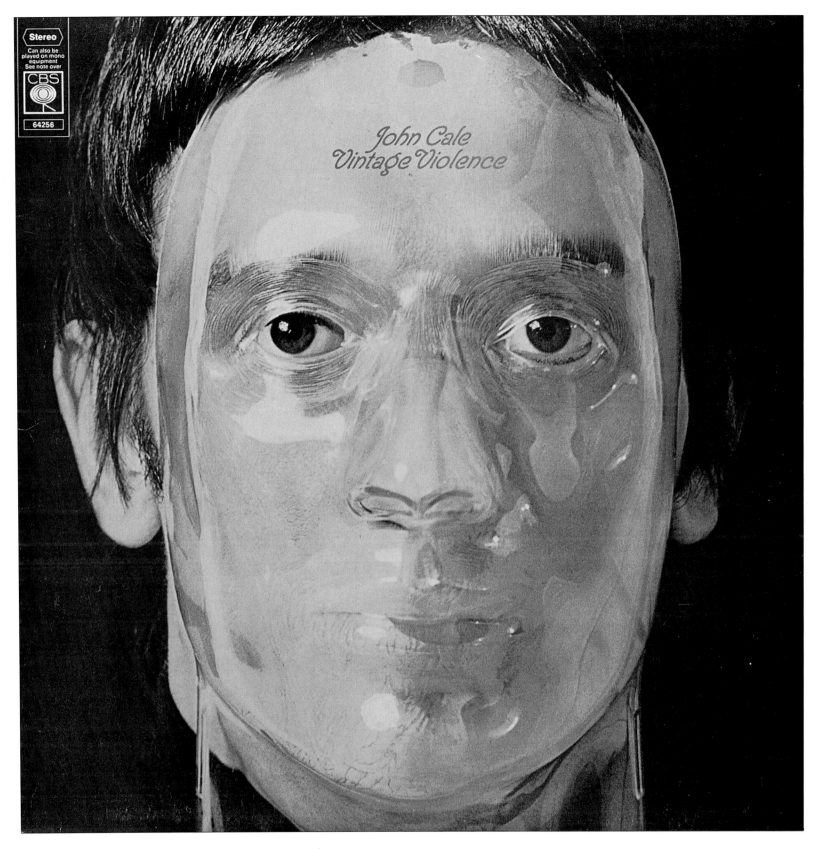

ARTISTE John Cale TITLE Vintage Violence DATE 1971 COMPANY CBS PHOTOGRAPHY Is Valeris

ARTISTE Santana TITLE Santana DATE 1971 COMPANY CBS DESIGN Heavy Water Light Show/Joan Chase & Mary Ann Mayer

ARTISTE The Beach Boys TITLE Surf's Up DATE 1971 COMPANY EMI (USA) DESIGN Ed Thrasher

BRITAIN GROPES IN THE DARK AS THE MINERS' STRIKE STARTS TO BITE

16 February The whole country was plunged into darkness for over nine hours yesterday when electricity cuts were imposed for the first time as the crisis over the miners' pay dispute deepens. Since last week, industry has been limited to working a three-day week in an attempt to restrict power consumption, and householders have been asked to heat only one room.

AUTOBIOGRAPHY OF HUGHES IS A HOAX

13 March One of the hoaxes of the century came to light today when writer Clifford Irving confessed to a New York court that he fabricated the 'autobiography' of the millionaire recluse Howard Hughes.

TERRORISTS MASSACRE TWENTY-SIX AT TEL AVIV AIRPORT

30 May Three Japanese killers launched a kamikaze terror raid on passengers at Tel Aviv airport late last night. Twenty-six people were killed, including a dozen Christian pilgrims to the Holy Land from Puerto Rico.

TOP RED ARMY TERRORIST CAPTURED

16 June Ulrike Meinhof, the last remaining member of the terrorist group the 'Red Army Faction' still at liberty, was captured in Hanover today. Over the last few weeks the bombing campaign of the Baader-Meinhof group has killed four people, seriously injured thirty-six and caused extensive damage to property.

BURGLARS CAUGHT IN WATERGATE OFFICES

17 June Five men were arrested at gunpoint in the Democratic National Committee's offices in the Watergate complex in Washington early this morning. Police say the men were attempting to 'bug' the opposition party headquarters with sophisticated electronic surveillance equipment, including miniature microphones.

PARATROOPERS FIRE ON DERRY MARCHERS

30 June An end to the conflict in Ulster seemed even more unlikely today, after British paratroopers opened fire when a civil rights march turned into a riot in Londonderry's Bogside area. Thirteen men and youths were killed and a further seventeen were wounded. The day was dubbed a 'Bloody Sunday' but Major-General Ford said the dead 'might not all have been killed by our troops'.

ANDES PLANE CRASH SURVIVORS ATE THE DEAD

29 December Sixteen survivors of a Uruguayan plane, which crashed in the Andes on 13 October, survived only by eating the flesh of other passengers who died in the crash. At a press conference in Montevideo, Sr Alfredo Delgado told journalists: 'If Jesus, in the Last Supper, offered his body and blood to the apostles, he was giving us to understand that we must do the same'.

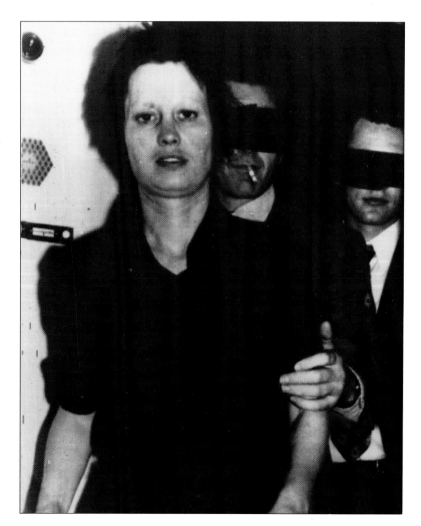

ARTISTE Emerson Lake & Palmer **TITLE** Brain Salad Surgery **COMPANY** Manticore (Atlantic) **DESIGN** Fabio Nicoli

SHEET MUSIC

ARTISTE 10cc TITLE Sheet Music COMPANY Decca DESIGN Hipgnosis

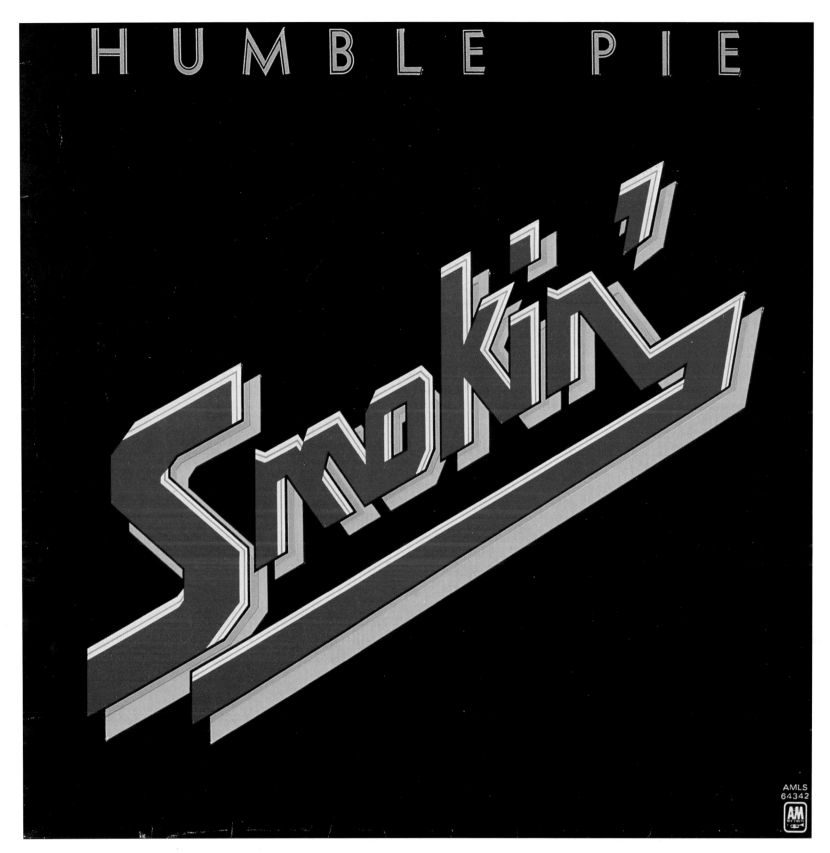

ARTISTE Humble Pie TITLE Smokin' DATE 1972 COMPANY A & M DESIGN John Kosh ILLUSTRATION Richard Eckford ART DIRECTION Mike Doud

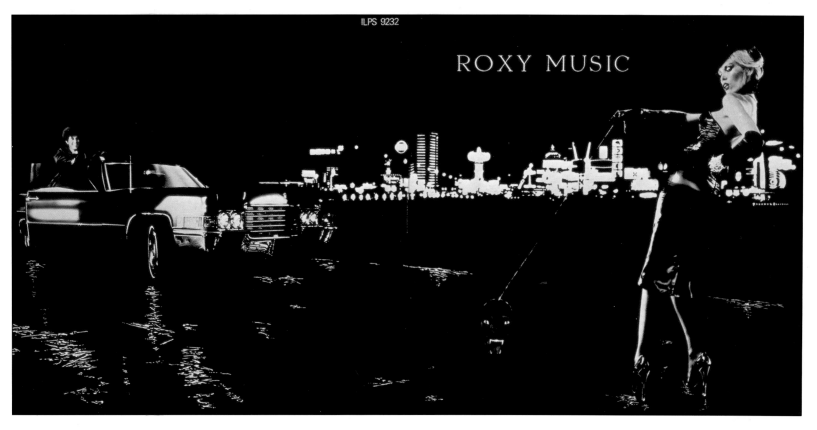

ARTISTE Roxy Music TITLE For Your Pleasure COMPANY Island COVER CONCEPT Brian Ferry PHOTOGRAPHY Karl Stoecker COPYRIGHT E.G. Records Ltd

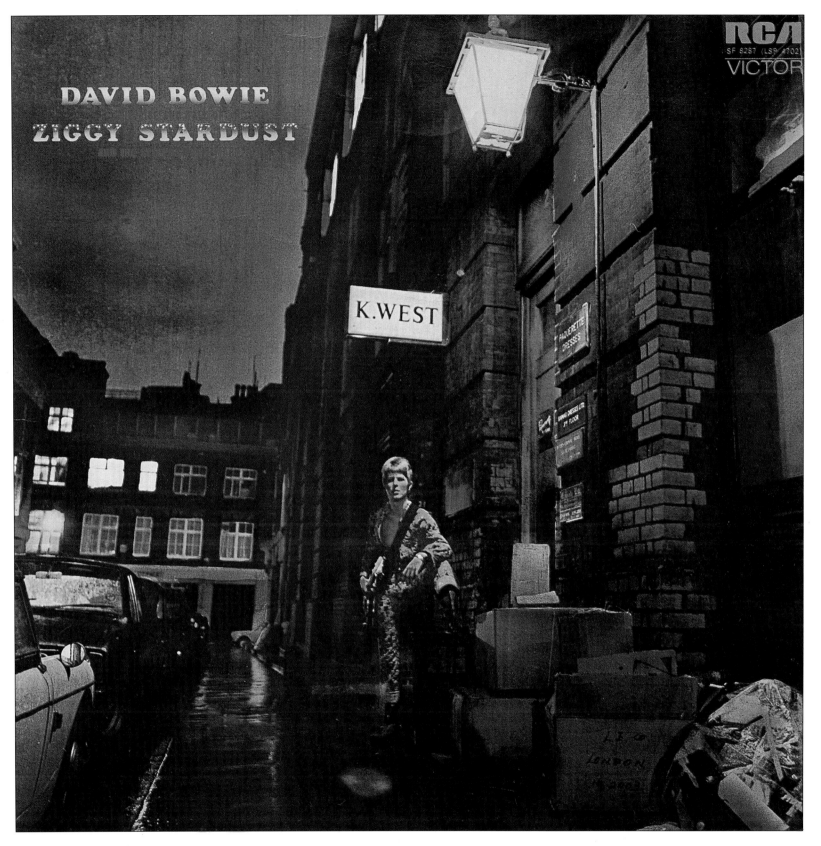

ARTISTE David Bowie TITLE Ziggy Stardust DATE 1972 COMPANY RCA ARTWORK Terry Pastor PHOTOGRAPHY Brian Ward

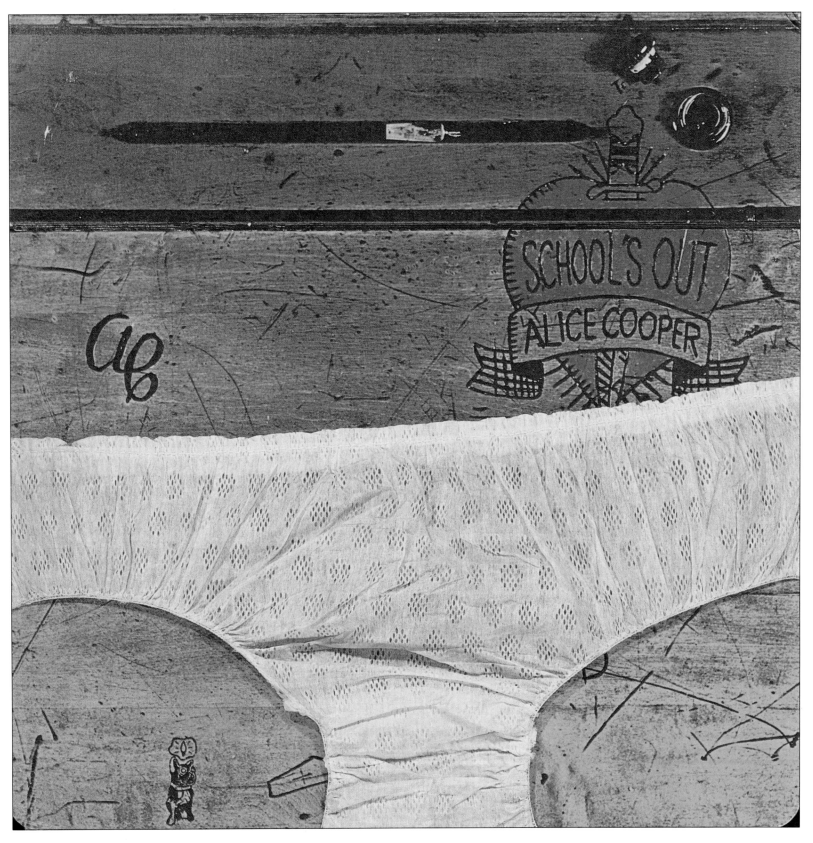

ARTISTE Alice Cooper TITLE School's Out DATE 1972 COMPANY Warner Bros DESIGN Wilkes and Braun Inc. PHOTOGRAPHY Robert Otter

ARTISTE Rolling Stones TITLE Exile On Main Street DATE 1972 COMPANY Rolling Stones DESIGN John Van Hamersveld/Norman Seeff PHOTOGRAPHY Robert Frank

ARTISTE Yes TITLE Close To The Edge DATE 1972 COMPANY Atlantic DESIGN Roger Dean

ARTISTE Tim Buckley TITLE Greetings From L.A. DATE 1972 COMPANY Warner Bros DESIGN Carl Schenkel

CAPTAIN BEEFHEART THE SPOTLIGHT KID

K44162

ARTISTE Captain Beefheart TITLE The Spotlight Kid DATE 1972 COMPANY Reprise (Kimney Record Group) DESIGN Ed Thrasher

ARTISTE Neil Young TITLE After The Gold Rush DATE 1972 COMPANY Reprise PHOTOGRAPHY Joel Bernstein

ARTISTE LSO Chamber Choir & Guest Soloists **TITLE** Tommy (The Who) **DATE** 1972 **COMPANY** A & M **DESIGN** Tom Wilkes/Wilkes/Braun

ARTISTE Santana TITLE Caravanserai DATE 1972 COMPANY CBS DESIGN Joan Chase

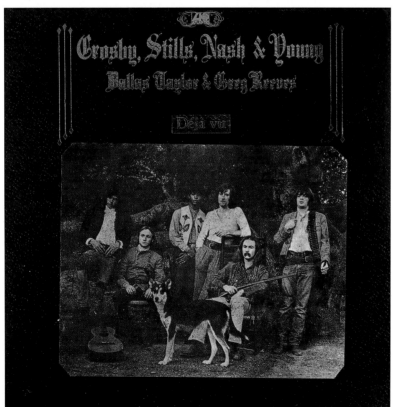

ARTISTE Fumble TITLE Fumble DATE 1972 COMPANY EMI (Sovereign) DESIGN Hipgnosis

ARTISTE Crosby, Stills, Nash & Young TITLE Deja Vu DATE 1972 COMPANY Atlantic
DESIGN Gary Burden PHOTOGRAPHY Tom Gundelfinger

ARTISTE Audience TITLE Lunch DATE 1972 COMPANY Charisma DESIGN Hipgnosis/Hardie

ARTISTE Jethro Tull TITLE Thick As A Brick DATE 1972 COMPANY Chrysalis

ISRAEL COUNTERS YOM KIPPUR OFFENSIVE

17 October Egyptian and Israeli troops were locked in one of the fiercest battles since World War II, eleven days after the Egyptians launched a shock attack across the Suez Canal on the holiest day in the Jewish calendar.

SHEIKS MASSIVELY INCREASE THE PRICE OF OIL

17 October The oil states sent shivers through the entire Western world today as they increased the price of a barrel of oil by over 70 per cent and at the same time cut back production in protest against the US support of Israel in the Yom Kippur War.

PRINCESS ANNE MARRIES

14 November Princess Anne walked to the high altar at Westminster Abbey on the arm of Prince Phillip to marry Captain Mark Phillips.

NIXON'S SECRETARY WIPES TAPE IN ERROR

26 November President Nixon's secretary gave evidence in court today that through some 'terrible mistake' she caused an eighteen-minute gap in one of the Watergate tapes. She told the court she pressed the wrong button, but was relieved when Nixon told her it did not matter.

BRITAIN GOES ON TO A THREE-DAY WEEK

17 December Describing the situation as 'the gravest by far since the end of the War', the Chancellor of the Exchequer, Anthony Barber, today cut a massive £1,200 million from public spending, including axing one in five of the schools and colleges due to be built in the next five years. Industry and commerce looks set to be limited to three days a week in the New Year, and all television services will close down at 10.30 p.m.

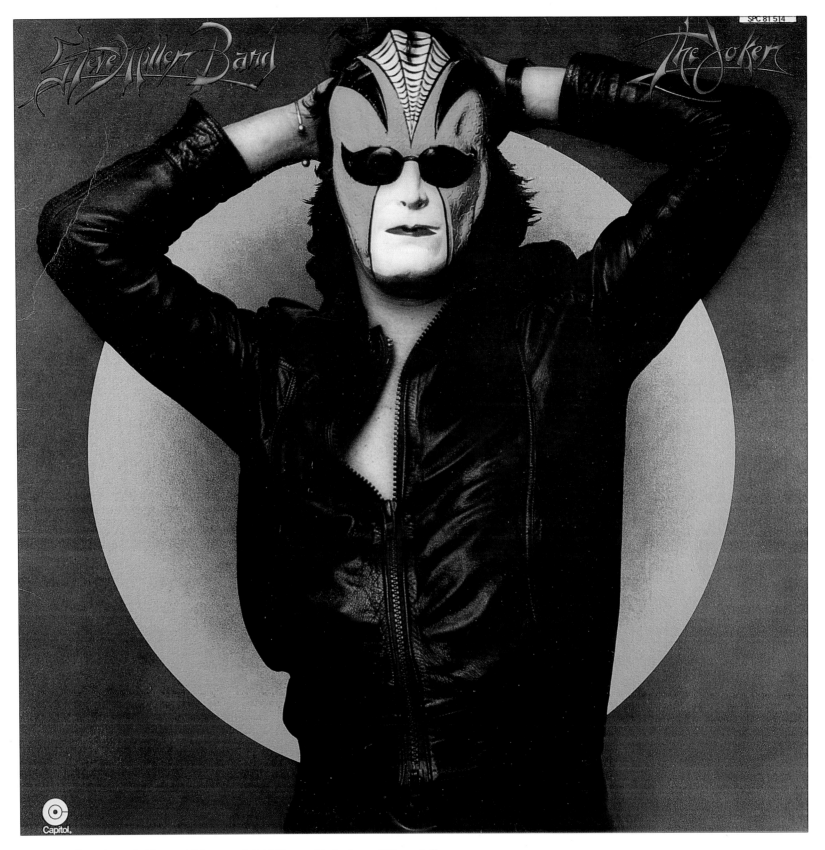

ARTISTE Steve Miller Band TITLE The Joker DATE 1973 COMPANY Capitol (EMI) DESIGN John Van Hamersveld/Norman Seeff

ARTISTE Mike Oldfield TITLE Tubular Bells DATE 1973 COMPANY Virgin PHOTOGRAPHY Trevor Key

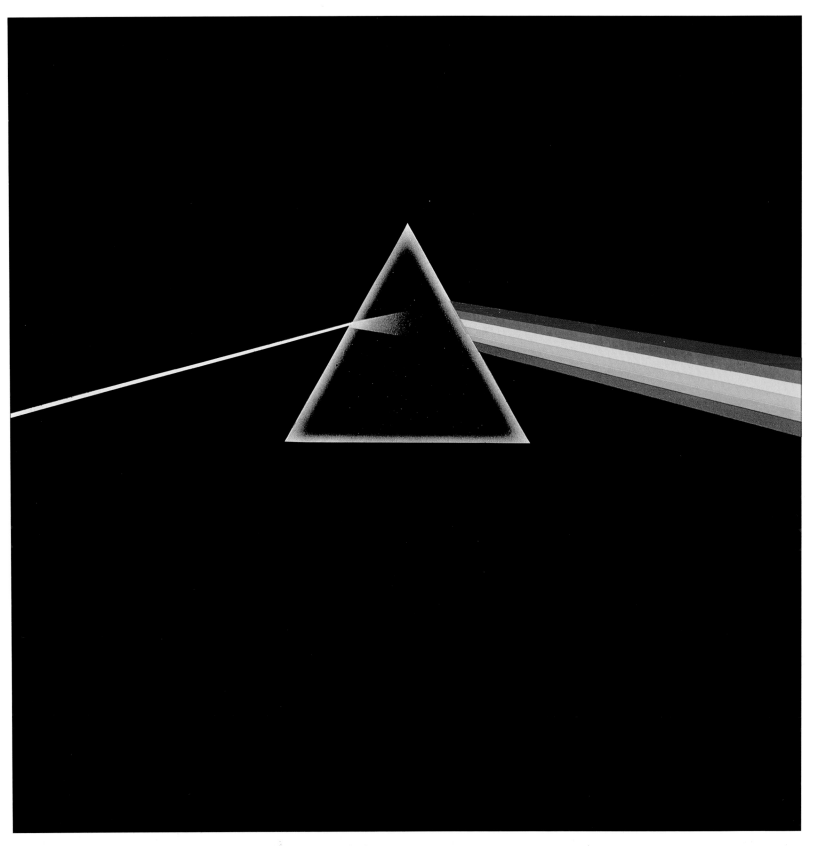

ARTISTE Pink Floyd TITLE Dark Side Of The Moon DATE 1973 COMPANY Harvest ARTWORK George Hardie NTA DESIGN Hipgnosis

ARTISTE The Doors **TITLE** Full Circle **COMPANY** Elektra/Asylum **DESIGN** Pacific Eye & Ear **ILLUSTRATION** Joe Garnett

ARTISTE Paul Kantner, Grace Slick & David Freiberg **TITLE** Baron Von Tollbooth & The Chrome Nun **DATE** 1973 **COMPANY** RCA (Grunt) **DESIGN** Pacific Eye & Ear **ILLUSTRATION** Drew Struzan

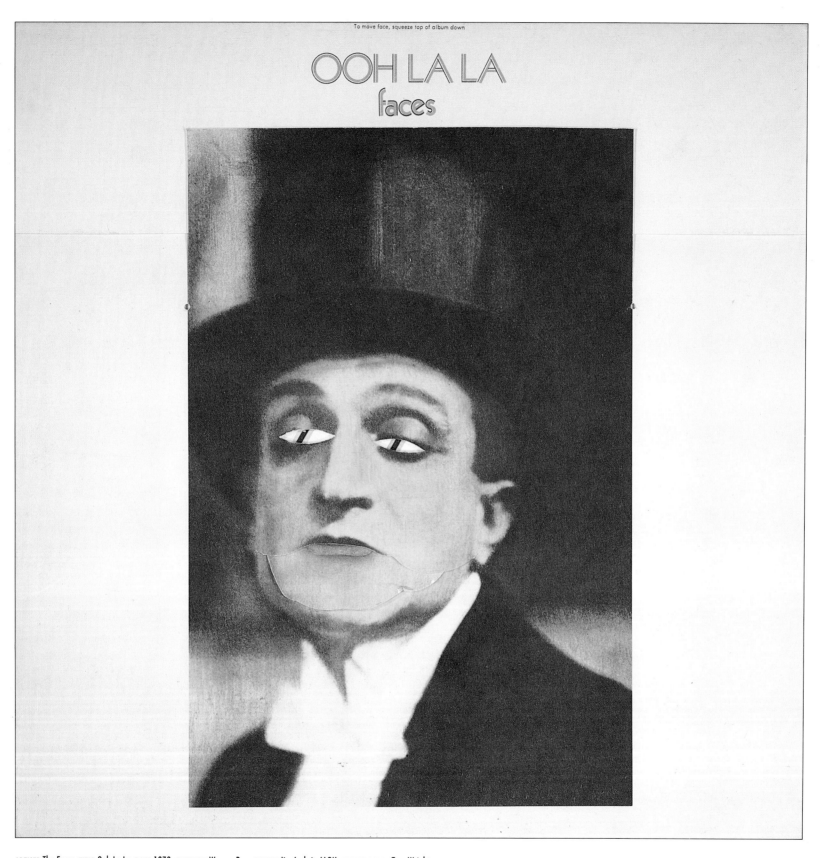

ARTISTE The Faces TITLE Ooh La La DATE 1973 COMPANY Warner Bros DESIGN Jim Ladwig (AGI) PHOTOGRAPHY Tom Wright

ARTISTE Shoot TITLE On The Frontier DATE 1973 COMPANY EMI DESIGN Fabio Nicoli Associates PHOTOGRAPHY Gered Mankowitz

ARTISTE Roxy Music TITLE Stranded DATE 1973 COMPANY Island COVER CONCEPT Bryan Ferry PHOTOGRAPHY Karl Stoecker COPYRIGHT E. G. Records Ltd

ARTISTE Led Zeppelin TITLE Houses Of The Holy DATE 1973 COMPANY Atlantic DESIGN Hipgnosis TINTING P. Crenell

ARTISTE Alice Cooper TITLE Billion Dollar Babies DATE 1973 COMPANY Warner Bros DESIGN Pacific Eye & Ear PHOTOGRAPHY David Bailey/Lynn Goldsmith/Neal Preston

ARTISTE The Wailers TITLE Catch A Fire DATE 1973 COMPANY Island DESIGN Rod Dyer/Bob Weiner

ARTISTE Van Morrison TITLE Hard Nose The Highway DATE 1973 COMPANY Warner Bros ILLUSTRATION Rob Springett

ARTISTE Todd Rundgren TITLE A Wizard/True Star DATE 1973 COMPANY Bearsville (Warner Bros) DESIGN Janson, Eding, Clapper

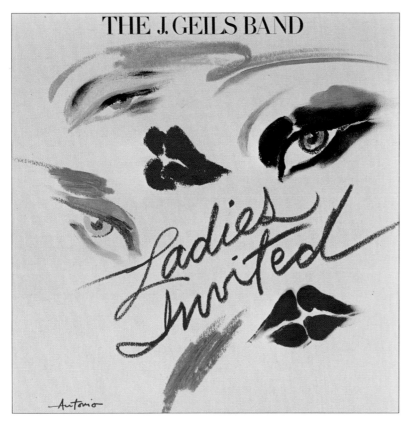

ARTISTE J. Geils Band TITLE Ladies Invited DATE 1973 COMPANY Atlantic DESIGN Ira Friedlander
ILLUSTRATION Antonio

ARTISTE Alice Cooper TITLE Muscle Of Love DATE 1973 COMPANY Warner Bros DESIGN Pacific Eye & Ear

ARTISTE David Bowie TITLE Aladdin Sane DATE 1973 COMPANY RCA
DESIGN Duffy & Celia Philo For Duffy Design Concepts

ARTISTE Iggy & The Stooges TITLE Raw Power DATE 1973 COMPANY CBS (Sony) PHOTOGRAPHY Mick Rock

ARTISTE Yes TITLE Tales From Topographic Oceans DATE 1973 COMPANY Atlantic DESIGN Roger Dean

ARTISTE Bruce Springsteen TITLE Greetings From Asbury Park N.J. DATE 1973 COMPANY CBS DESIGN John Berg PHOTOGRAPHY Courtesy Tichnor Bros Inc. Boston

DR SPOCK BLAMED FOR REVOLTING YOUTH

23 January Dr Benjamin Spock, whose best-selling book The Common Sense Book of Baby and Child Care has been the paediatric 'bible' for millions on both sides of the Atlantic, was blamed today for much of the contemporary youth rebellion. Many critics suggest that the ills of the so-called 'permissive society' are the result of Dr Spock's influential and controversial teachings. But doctors insists that his original theories, which suggest parents relax their control and let kids have their own way, have been misinterpreted.

AUTHOR SOLZHENITSYN SENT INTO EXILE

14 February Alexander Solzhenitsyn was expelled from his homeland and deprived of his Soviet citizenship today. This was a result of his recent revelations about conditions in Soviet labour camps under Lenin and Stalin in his book The Gulag Archipelago.

HEATH SEEKS DEAL WITH THORPE TO HANG ON TO POWER

1 March In a political crisis, Conservative Prime Minister Heath told the Queen tonight that he will try to negotiate with Liberal leader Jeremy Thorpe over the weekend for support. If he fails, Mr Heath will resign and Labour will be back in power.

HUGE CHEMICAL EXPLOSION AT FLIXBOROUGH

2 June Twenty-nine people were killed today in a massive explosion in the tiny community of Flixborough on Humberside. The village had only recently overcome fears of the danger of the plant as a result of the employment prospects offered by the company.

NIXON, FIRST US PRESIDENT TO RESIGN

8 August President Richard Nixon today announced his resignation. He faces imminent impeachment by Congress for 'high crimes and misde-meanours' in the Watergate scandal.

JAPANESE CAR SALES GO INTO OVERDRIVE

15 September For the first time foreign cars are outselling the British Leyland range. Figures just released indicate that foreign cars took a record 32 per cent of the British market.

POLICE HUNT LORD LUCAN IN NANNY'S MURDER

12 November Richard John Bingham, the Seventh Earl of Lucan but known to his chums in London's gaming society as 'Lucky', is being sought by police in connection with the brutal murder of his nanny, 29-year-old Sandra Rivett, and an attack on his estranged wife.

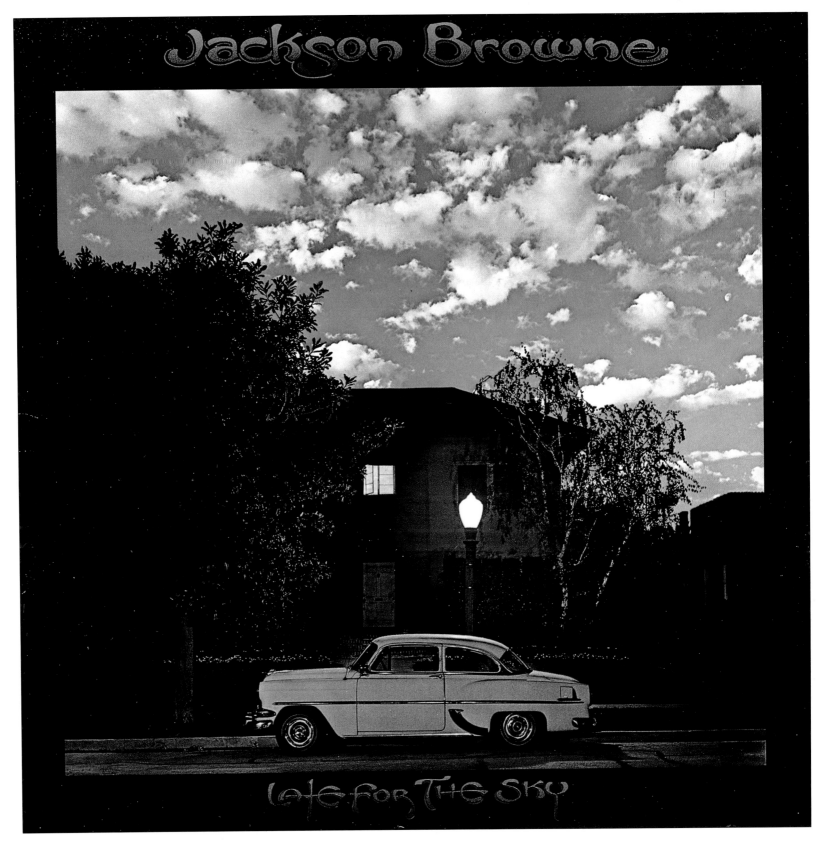

ARTISTE Jackson Browne TITLE Late For The Sky DATE 1974 COMPANY Elektra/Asylum PHOTOGRAPHY Bob Seidemann TYPOGRAPHY Rick Griffin

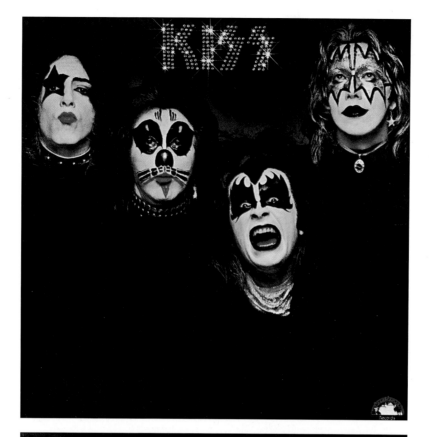

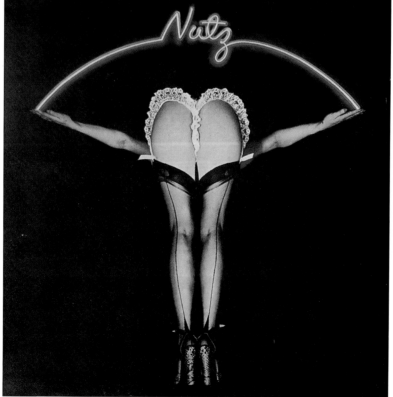

ARTISTE Kiss TITLE Kiss DATE 1974 COMPANY Casablanca DESIGN Lockart; Joel Brodsky

ARTISTE Nutz TITLE Nutz DATE 1974 COMPANY A & M DESIGN Geoff Halpin

ARTISTE Ted Nugent's Amboy Dukes TITLE Tooth Fang & Claw DATE 1974 COMPANY Discreet (Warner Bros)
DESIGN J. Flournoy Holmes (Wonder Graphics)

ARTISTE Rolling Stones TITLE Made In The Shade DATE 1974 COMPANY Rolling Stones DESIGN Christian Piper

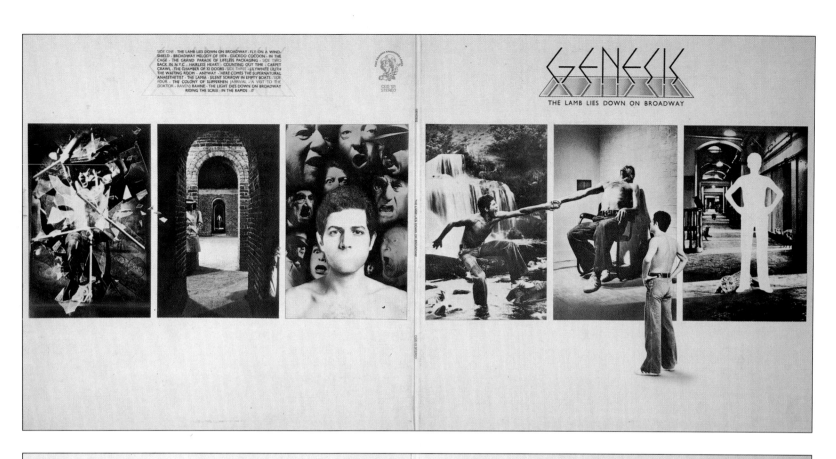

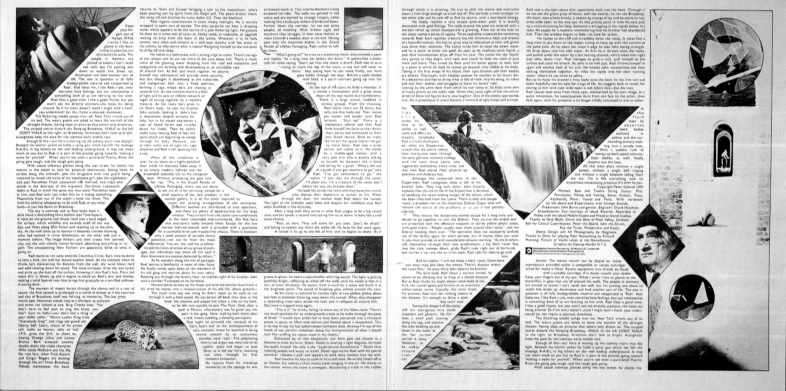

ARTISTE Genesis **TITLE** The Lamb Lies Down On Broadway **DATE** 1974 **COMPANY** Charisma **DESIGN & PHOTOGRAPHY** Hipgnosis

ARTISTE Pretty Things **TITLE** Silk Torpedo **DATE** 1974 **COMPANY** Swan Song **DESIGN** Hipgnosis

BLUE ÖYSTER CULT
SECRET TREATIES

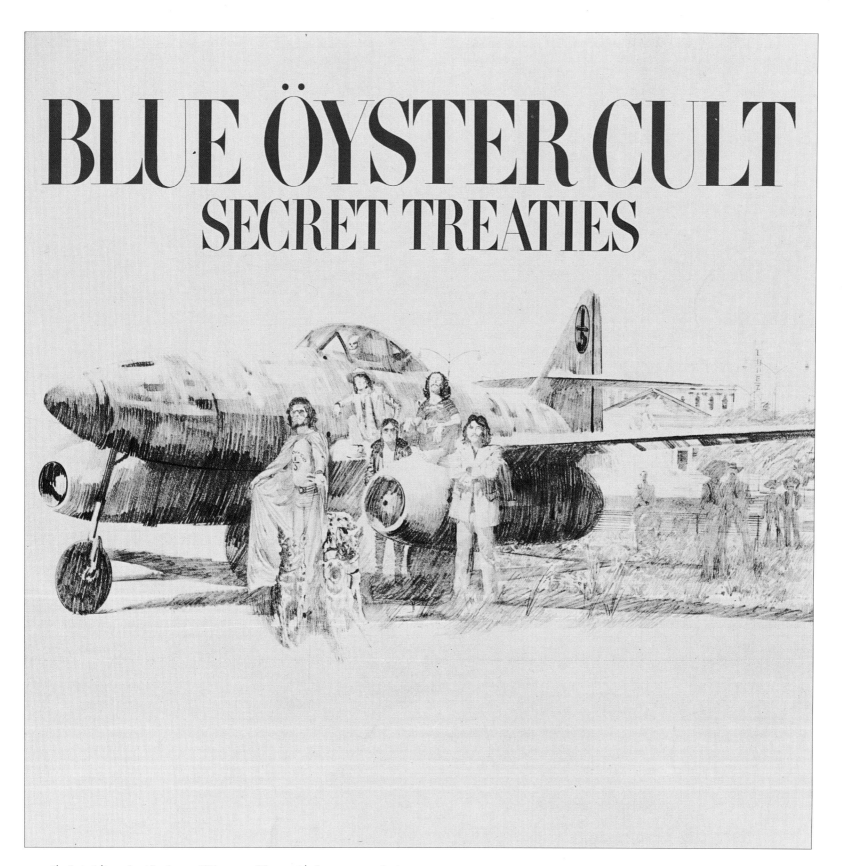

ARTISTE Blue Oyster Cult TITLE Secret Treaties DATE 1974 COMPANY CBS DESIGN John Berg ILLUSTRATION Ron Lesser

ARTISTE Deep Purple TITLE Stormbringer DATE 1974 COMPANY EMI DESIGN John Cabalka ART DIRECTION Ed Thrasher ILLUSTRATION Joe Garnett

ARTISTE Supertramp TITLE Crime Of The Century DATE 1974 COMPANY A & M ART DIRECTION Fabia Nicoli PHOTOGRAPHY Paul Wakefield

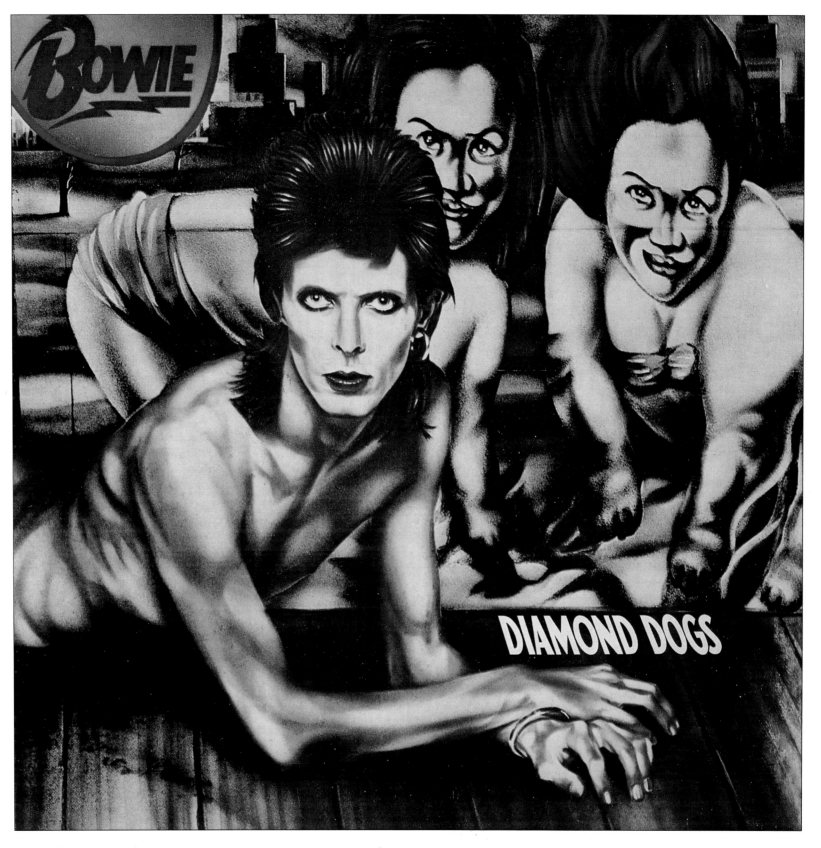

ARTISTE David Bowie TITLE Diamond Dogs DATE 1974 COMPANY RCA ART DIRECTION AGI ARTWORK Guy Peellaert

ROXY MUSIC

ARTISTE Roxy Music TITLE Country Life DATE 1974 COMPANY ATCO (USA) COVER CONCEPT Bryan Ferry PHOTOGRAPHY Eric Boman COPYRIGHT E.G. Records Ltd

ARTISTE Robert Palmer TITLE Sneakin' Sally Through The Alley DATE 1974 COMPANY Island PHOTOGRAPHY Graham Hughes

ARTISTE Santana TITLE Borboletta DATE 1974 COMPANY CBS DESIGN Carlos Santana & Barry Imhoff

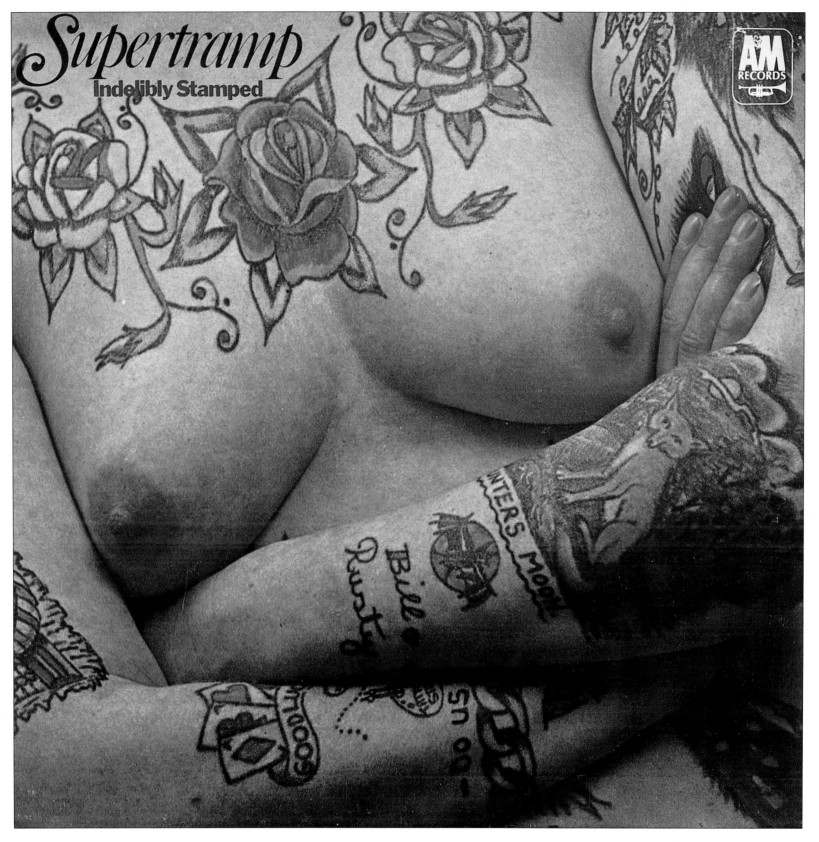

ARTISTE Supertramp TITLE Indelibly Stamped DATE 1974 COMPANY A & M DESIGN Bob Hook PHOTOGRAPHY Keith Morris

ARTISTE Yes TITLE Relayer DATE 1974 COMPANY Atlantic DESIGN Roger Dean

SEVENTH WAVE

THINGS TO COME

ARTISTE Seventh Wave TITLE Things To Come DATE 1974 COMPANY Gull DESIGN David Howells ILLUSTRATION Michael Priddle TYPOGRAPHY Richard Rockwood

ARTISTE Eddie Harris TITLE Is It In DATE 1974 COMPANY Atlantic (USA) ILLUSTRATION Peter Palombi

ARTISTE The Tubes TITLE The Tubes COMPANY A & M
DESIGN M. Cotten, P. Prince (Airamid Designs) PHOTOGRAPHY Harry Mittman

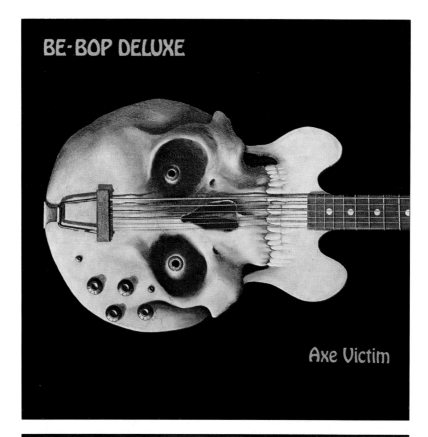

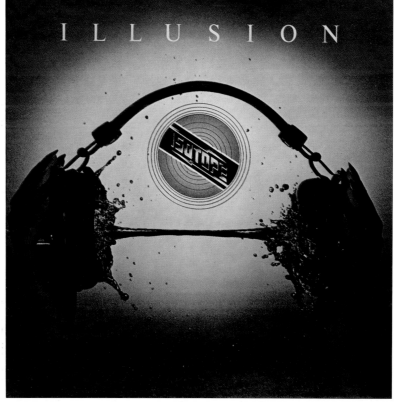

ARTISTE Be-Bop Deluxe TITLE Axe Victim DATE 1974 COMPANY Harvest
DESIGN & PHOTOGRAPHY Mick Rock PAINTING John Holmes

ARTISTE Isotope TITLE Illusion DATE 1974 COMPANY Gull DESIGN John Pasche, Gull Graphics
PHOTOGRAPHY Phil Jude

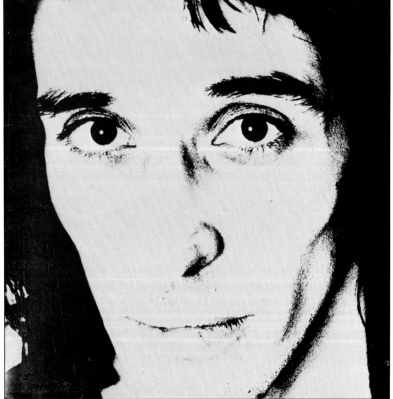

ARTISTE Jerry Garcia TITLE Garcia DATE 1974 COMPANY Round Recs (Warner Bros) DESIGN Mascoso

ARTISTE John Cale TITLE Fear DATE 1974 COMPANY Island PHOTOGRAPHY Keith Morris

ARTISTE Mott the Hoople TITLE The Hoople DATE 1974 COMPANY Island DESIGN Roslav Szaybo PHOTOGRAPHY John Brown MODEL Kari Ann

ARTISTE UFO TITLE Phenomenon DATE 1974 COMPANY Chrysalis DESIGN Hipgnosis COLOURING Maurice Tate

ARTISTE Fleetwood Mac TITLE Heroes Are Hard To Find DATE 1974 COMPANY Reprise
DESIGN Des Strobel/AGI PHOTOGRAPHY Herbert Worthington

ARTISTE Neil Young TITLE On The Beach DATE 1974 COMPANY Reprise DESIGN Gary Burden

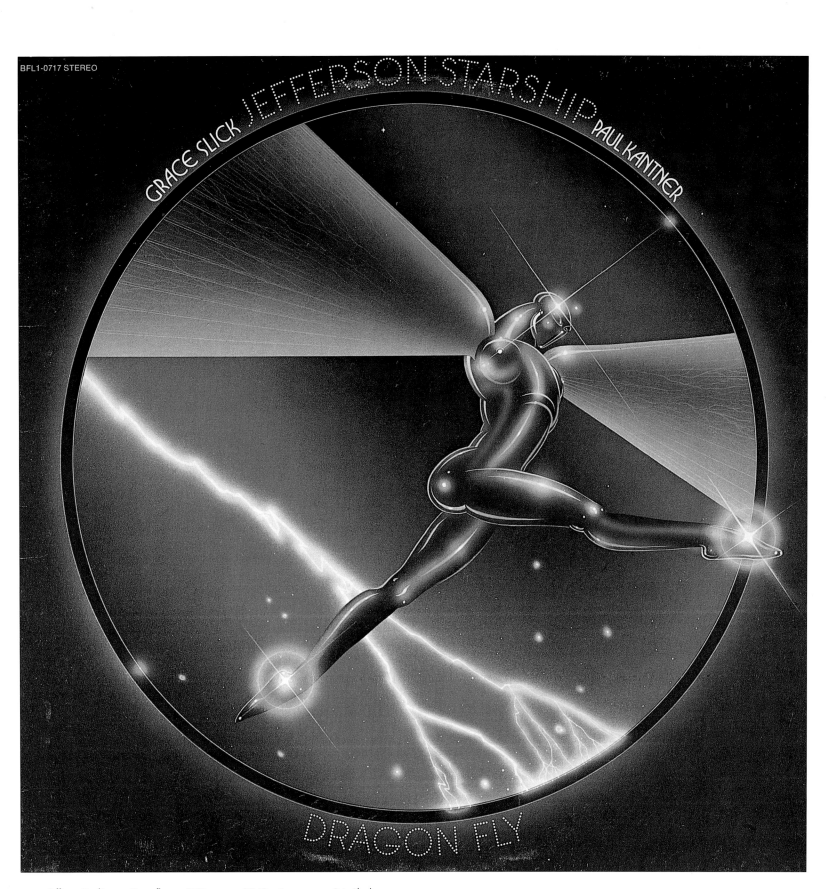

ARTISTE Jefferson Starship TITLE Dragonfly DATE 1974 COMPANY RCA (Grunt) ILLUSTRATION Peter Lloyd

WEATHER REPORT

MYSTERIOUS TRAVELLER

ARTISTE Weather Report **TITLE** Mysterious Traveller **DATE** 1974 **COMPANY** CBS **DESIGN** Teresa Alfieri **ARTWORK** Helmot K. Wmmer & The American Museum Hyden Planetarium

ARTISTE Santana TITLE Greatest Hits DATE 1974 COMPANY CBS DESIGN John Berg PHOTOGRAPHY Joel Baldwin

ARTISTE Roy Wood TITLE Mustard COMPANY United Artists DESIGN Beverley Parker

UNEMPLOYMENT HITS THE MILLION MARK

24 April According to figures released today the number out of work in Britain has passed the million mark, in the biggest monthly increase since the World War II.

PANIC AT US EMBASSY AS SAIGON FALLS

31 April The war in Vietnam is over. North Vietnamese tanks rolled down the avenues of Saigon this morning and, meeting almost no resistance, knocked down the gates of the presidential palace. All the Americans have finally departed in a last-minute airlift from the roof of the Embassy, as masses of people swarmed around it, desperate to get a place on the helicopters ferrying the last of the foreigners and well-connected Vietnamese to US warships waiting off the coast.

QUEEN OPENS NORTH SEA PIPELINE

3 November Queen Elizabeth II today opened the first pipeline to bring oil from the newly built BP Forties Field, more than 100 miles (160km) along the seabed to a refinery on the Firth of Forth. When production reaches expected levels the pipeline will supply about 400,000 barrels a day, about one-quarter of Britain's oil requirement. Prime Minister Harold Wilson, who was at today's ceremony, said: 'We expect to be self-sufficient in oil by 1980.'

FRANCO DIES – MONARCHY RETURNS TO SPAIN

22 November Don Juan Carlos Borbon y Borbon was sworn in before the Spanish Parliament today as the first occupant of the Spanish throne since 1931. With Franco gone, Spain faces an uncertain future.

ARTISTE Sparks **TITLE** Indiscreet **DATE** 1975 **COMPANY** Island **PHOTOGRAPHY** Richard Creamer

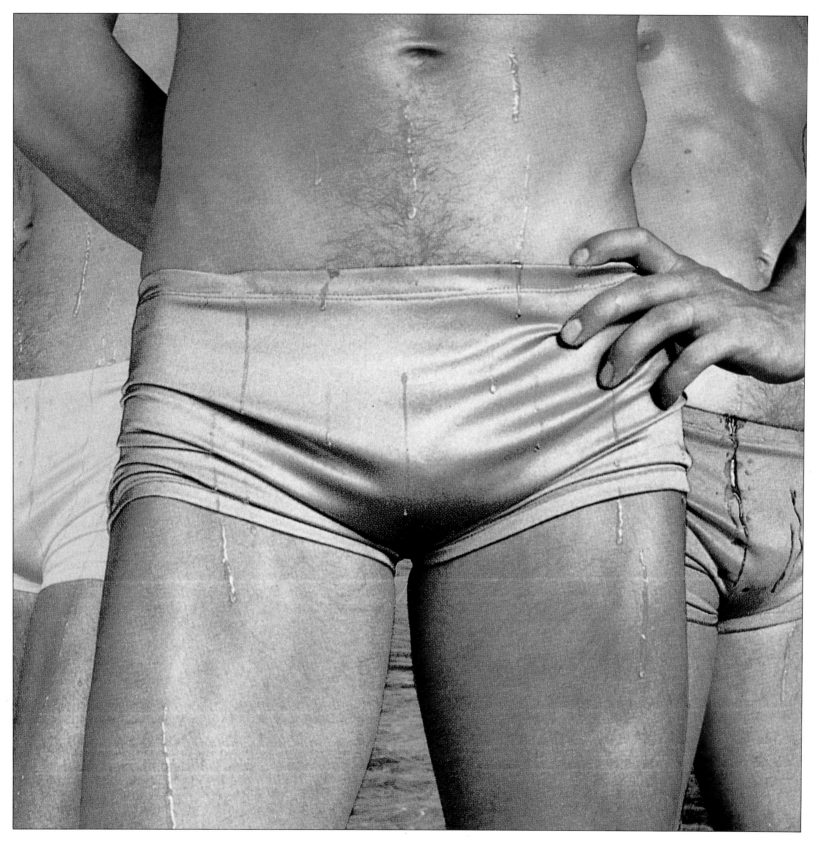

ARTISTE The Winkies TITLE The Winkies DATE 1975 COMPANY Chrysalis DESIGN Hipgnosis

ARTISTE Grateful Dead **TITLE** Blues For Allah **DATE** 1975 **COMPANY** Grateful Dead **ILLUSTRATION** Philip Garris

ARTISTE Edgar Winter TITLE The Edgar Winter Band With Rick Derringer DATE 1975 COMPANY Blue Sky PHOTOGRAPHY Hiro

ARTISTE Pink Floyd TITLE Wish You Were Here DATE 1975 COMPANY EMI (Harvest) DESIGN Hipgnosis

ARTISTE Electric Light Orchestra TITLE Face The Music DATE 1975 COMPANY Jet DESIGN John Kehe/Mick Haggerty (Art Attack) PHOTOGRAPHY Fred Valentine

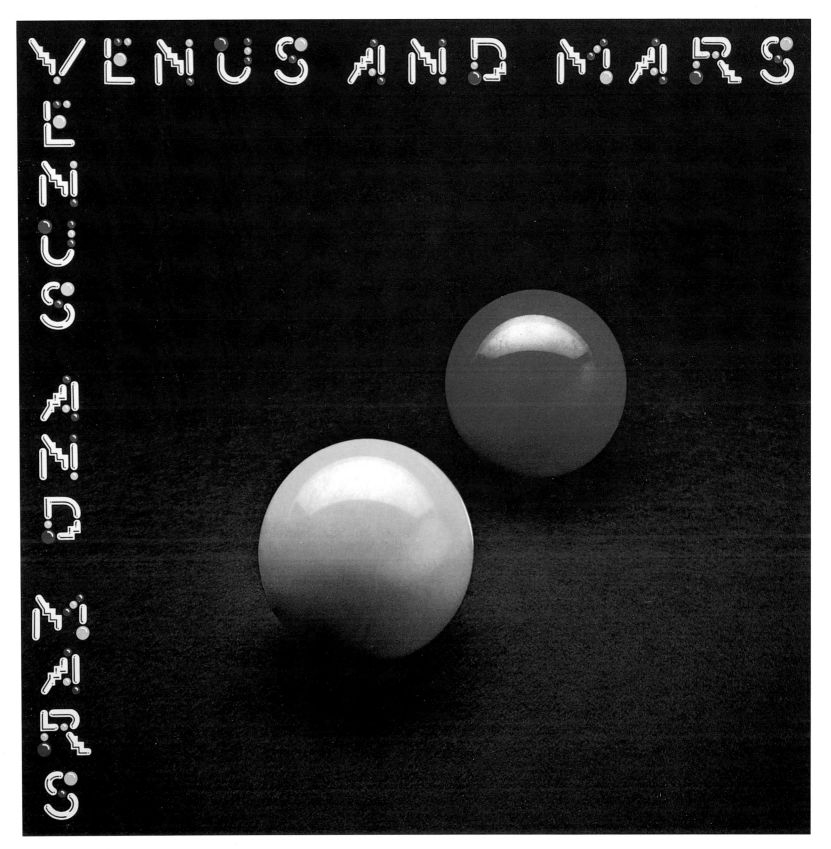

ARTISTE Wings TITLE Venus And Mars DATE 1975 COMPANY EMI DESIGN Hipgnosis/Paul and Linda McCartney

ARTISTE Linda Ronstadt TITLE Hasten Down The Wind COMPANY Elektra/Asylum DESIGN John Kosh
PHOTOGRAPHY Ethan Russell & Jim Shea

ARTISTE Carly Simon TITLE Playing Possum DATE 1975 COMPANY Elektra/Asylum PHOTOGRAPHY Norman Seeff

ARTISTE Roger Daltrey TITLE Ride A Rock Horse DATE 1975 COMPANY Goldhawke
ART DIRECTION, CONCEPT & PHOTOGRAPHY Graham Hughes

ARTISTE Shawn Phillips TITLE Do You Wonder DATE 1975 COMPANY A & M
DESIGN Junie Osaki/John Cabalka PHOTOGRAPHY Leonard Koren

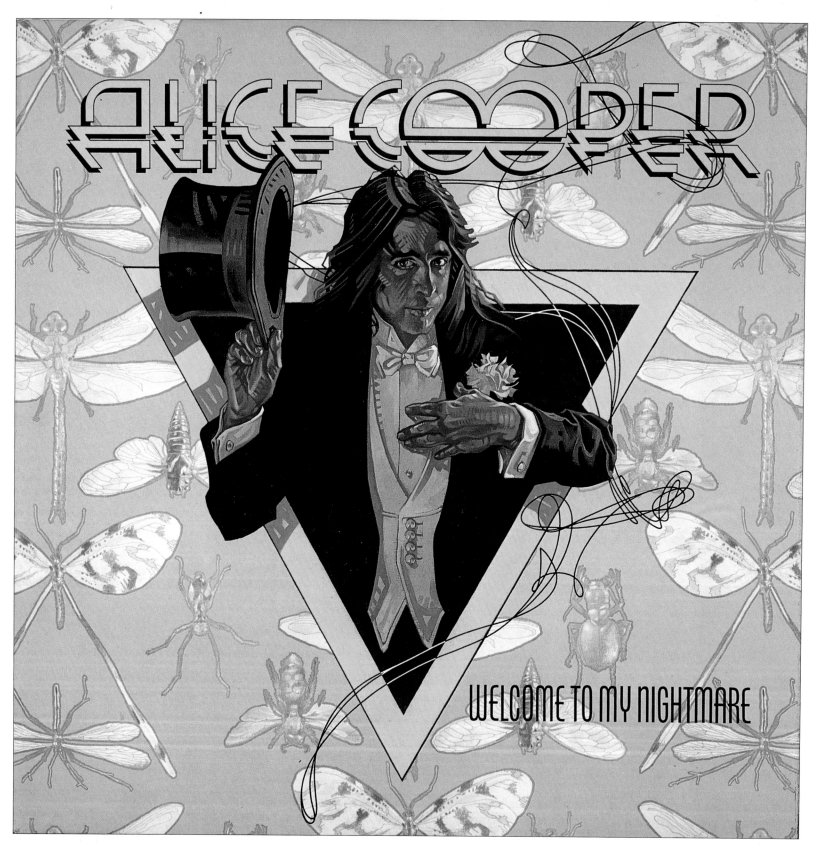

ARTISTE Alice Cooper TITLE Welcome To My Nightmare DATE 1975 COMPANY Atlantic DESIGN Pacific Eye & Ear ILLUSTRATION Drew Struzan PHOTOGRAPHY Bret Lopez

TROUT MASK REPLICA

CAPTAIN BEEFHEART
& HIS MAGIC BAND

ARTISTE Captain Beefheart TITLE Trout Mask Replica DATE 1975 COMPANY Warner Bros (Reprise) DESIGN Cal Schenkel PHOTOGRAPHY Ed Caraeff/Cal Schenkel

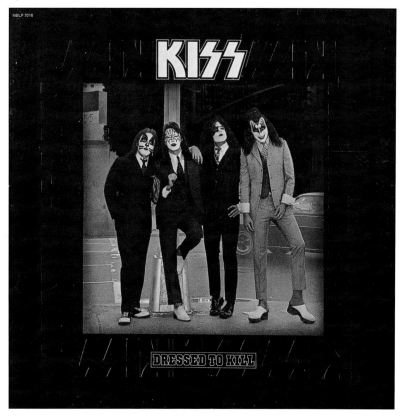

ARTISTE Kiss **TITLE** Dressed To Kill **DATE** 1975 **COMPANY** Casablanca **DESIGN** Peter Corriston
PHOTOGRAPHY Bob Gruen

ARTISTE Fleetwood Mac **TITLE** Fleetwood Mac **DATE** 1975 **COMPANY** Reprise **DESIGN** Des Strobel/AGI
PHOTOGRAPHY Herbert Worthington **CONCEPT** Fleetwood Mac

ARTISTE UFO **TITLE** Force It **DATE** 1975 **COMPANY** Chrysalis (USA)
DESIGN & PHOTOGRAPHY Hipgnosis

ARTISTE Eno **TITLE** Another Green World **DATE** 1975 **COMPANY** Polydor **ILLUSTRATION** Tom Phillips
TYPOGRAPHY Bob Bowkett/C.C.S.

ARTISTE Journey TITLE Journey DATE 1975 COMPANY CBS DESIGN Nancy Donald PHOTOGRAPHY Steven Silverstein

ARTISTE Isotope TITLE Deep End DATE 1975 COMPANY Gull DESIGN John Pasche for Gull Graphics TYPOGRAPHY John Pasche PHOTOGRAPHY Phil Jude

PATTY HEARST GUILTY OF ARMED ROBBERY

19 March Patricia Hearst, heir to the fortune of media magnate Randolph Hearst, was found guilty today of helping her kidnappers, the so-called Symbionese Liberation Army, in an armed bank robbery. The jury in the San Francisco court remained unimpressed by her claims that she was brainwashed by her captors, who allegedly held her in a broom cupboard for weeks at a time.

US IN GRIP OF BICENTENNIAL FEVER

4 July America celebrated its 200th birthday today with a display of lasers in Washington, cheered on by an audience of over a million people. But Vice-President Rockerfeller warned that the country's problems might be 'insurmountable'.

EARTHMEN GET CLOSE LOOK AT MARS

20 July The first close-up pictures of the surface of Mars were received this morning from the American spacecraft Viking, which landed after an eleven-month journey through space. The craft will be analysing soil, and searching for signs of life.

'RACE RIOT' MARS NOTTING HILL CARNIVAL

31 August The traditional annual Bank Holiday Caribbean carnival ended in fierce race riots as police and youths held a pitched battle on the usually placid streets of Notting Hill. Hundreds were hurt, as cars and buildings were looted and set on fire.

CHAT SHOW HOST SUSPENDED IN SEX PISTOLS TV ROW

3 December Thames TV presenter Bill Grundy was suspended after his early evening Today show featured the 'enfants terribles' of rock, the Sex Pistols. During the programme on Punk music, of which the band are the leading exponents, one of the band uttered an expletive. When Grundy unwisely asked him to repeat it the programme deteriorated into what Grundy described as a 'tirade by a foul-mouthed set of yobs'. Malcolm McLaren, manager of the Sex Pistols, agreed the band were yobs 'and proud of it'.

ARTISTE Led Zeppelin TITLE Presence DATE 1976 COMPANY Swan Song DESIGN George Hardie & Hipgnosis

ARTISTE The James Montgomery Band **TITLE** The James Montgomery Band **DATE** 1976 **COMPANY** Island **DESIGN** Mike Fink/Rod Dyer Inc. **ILLUSTRATION** Mick Haggerty

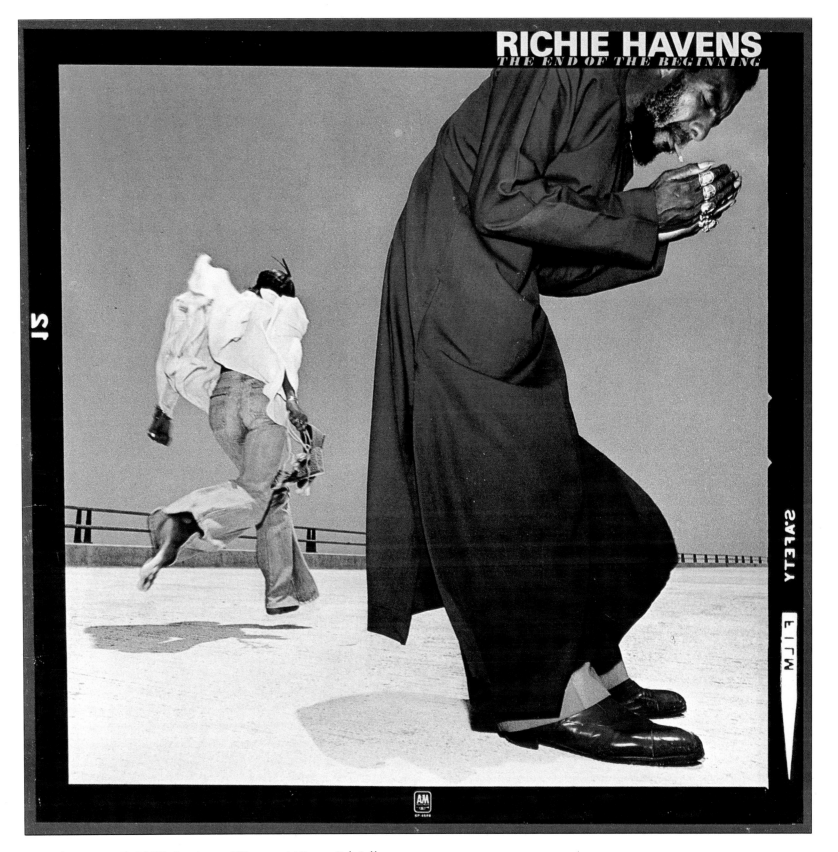

ARTISTE Richie Havens **TITLE** The End Of The Beginning **DATE** 1976 **COMPANY** A & M **DESIGN** Moshe Brakha

ARTISTE Boz Scaggs **TITLE** Silk Degrees **DATE** 1976 **COMPANY** CBS **DESIGN** Nancy Donald & Ron Coro **PHOTOGRAPHY** Moshe Brakha

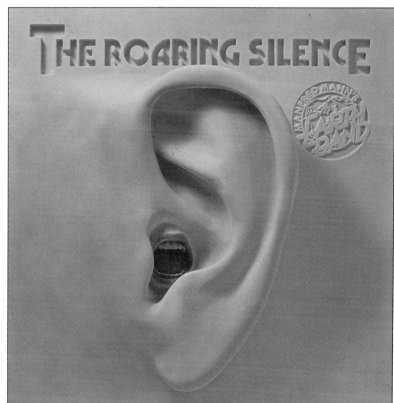

ARTISTE Be-Bop Deluxe TITLE Sunburst Finish DATE 1976 COMPANY Harvest (EMI) DESIGN Mike Doud

ARTISTE Manfred Mann's Earth Band TITLE The Roaring Silence DATE 1976 COMPANY Bronze
DESIGN Shirtsleeves Studios

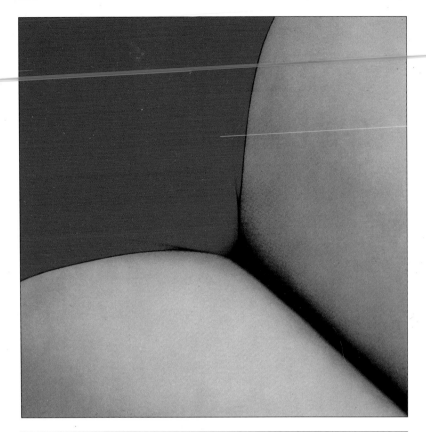

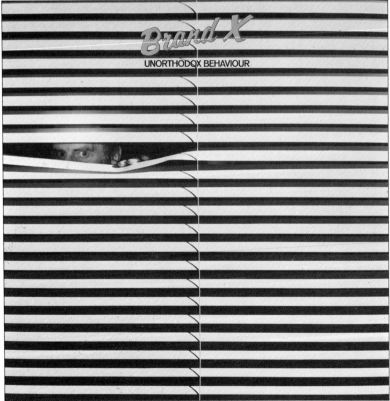

ARTISTE Montrose TITLE Jump On It DATE 1976 COMPANY Warner Bros DESIGN Hipgnosis

ARTISTE Brand X TITLE Unorthodox Behaviour DATE 1976 COMPANY Charisma DESIGN Hipgnosis

ARTISTE Dave Greenslade TITLE Cactus Choir DATE 1976 COMPANY Warner Bros DESIGN Roger Dean

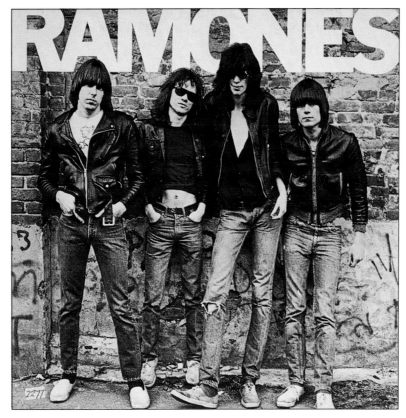

ARTISTE Ramones TITLE Ramones DATE 1976 COMPANY Sire PHOTOGRAPHY Roberta Bayley (Punk Magazine)

ARTISTE Roogalator TITLE All Aboard DATE 1976 COMPANY Stiff PHOTOGRAPHY J.I. Bajzert DESIGN Edward Barker

ARTISTE Eddie And The Hot Rods TITLE Teenage Depression DATE 1976 COMPANY Island PHOTOGRAPHY Michael Beal

'LET'S DO IT' SAYS GARY GILMORE

17 January Murderer Gary Gilmore, one of the few residents of Death Row in ten years to request he be executed, finally got his wish this morning. With the words 'let's do it', he stepped out in front of a firing squad at the Utah State Prison, so ending a lengthy nationwide campaign against the death penalty.

ELVIS DEAD

16 August Elvis Aaron Presley, for more than twenty years the undisputed 'King' of rock 'n' roll, was found dead today in Graceland, the mansion in Memphis where he lived. First reports suggest that his death was due to a drug overdose, and rumour has it that the King was fatally addicted to tranquillizers and barbiturates.

SKYTRAIN PROMISES REVOLUTION IN AIR TRAVEL

26 September Sir Freddie Laker launched his cut-price no-frills 'Skytrain' service from Gatwick to New York. Passengers, some of whom had queued for twenty-four hours to get one of the £59 tickets, were personally thanked by Sir Freddie for 'helping to prove me right'.

SOUTH AFRICAN POLICE CLEARED OF BIKO DEATH

2 December South African Black Consciousness leader Steve Biko, interrogated for five days, during which he was kept naked and manacled in a police cell at Port Elizabeth, was found unconscious and foaming at the mouth. He was then driven 750 miles (1,200km) to Pretoria where he died of brain injuries in a prison hospital. A magistrate today ruled that police could not be held responsible for his death.

ARTISTE The Sex Pistols TITLE Never Mind The Bollocks Here's The Sex Pistols DATE 1977 COMPANY Virgin DESIGN Jamie Reid

ARTISTE The Jam TITLE In The City DATE 1977 COMPANY Polydor DESIGN Bill Smith PHOTOGRAPHY Martin Goddard

ARTISTE 999 TITLE Nasty Nasty DATE 1977 COMPANY United Artists
DESIGN George 'God' Snow (Green Vinyl)

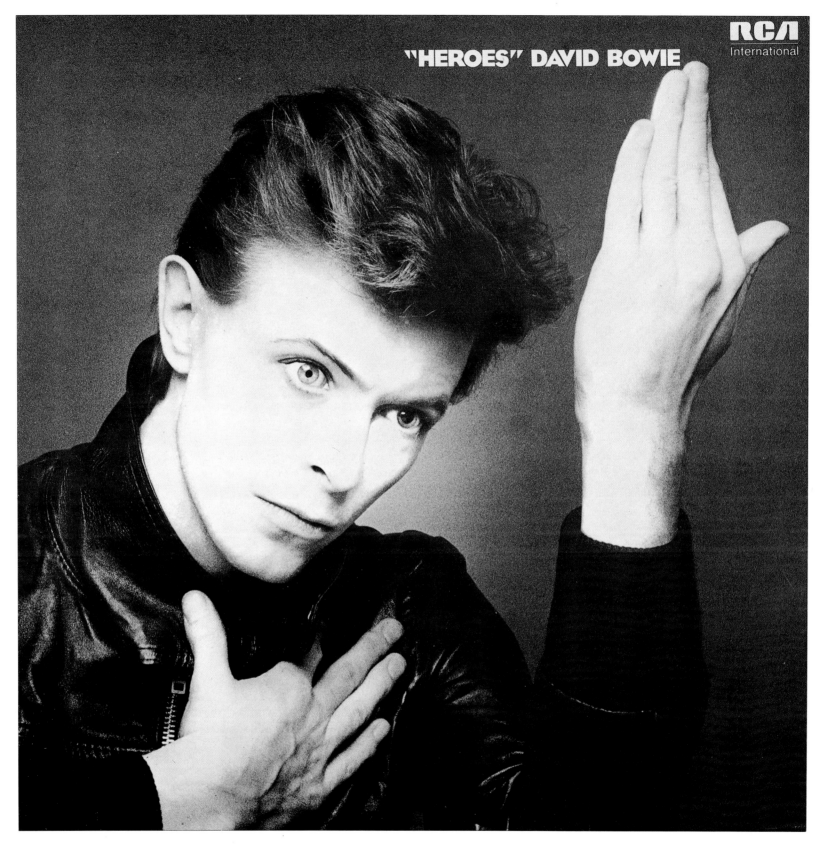

ARTISTE David Bowie TITLE Heroes DATE 1977 COMPANY RCA PHOTOGRAPHY Sukita

ARTISTE The Clash TITLE The Clash DATE 1977 COMPANY CBS DESIGN J. Guttner
PHOTO Kate Simon ART DIRECTION Roslav Szaybo

ARTISTE The Sex Pistols TITLE God Save The Queen DATE 1977 COMPANY Virgin
DESIGN & ILLUSTRATION Jamie Reid

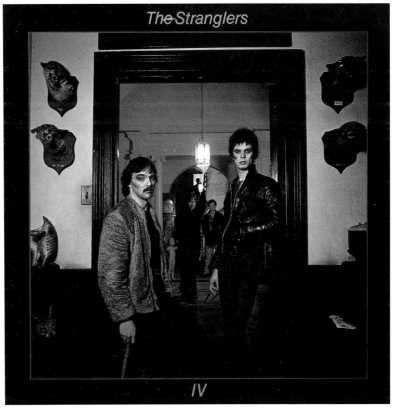

ARTISTE Kraftwerk TITLE Trans Europe Express DATE 1977 COMPANY Capitol PHOTOGRAPHY J. Stara Paris
CONCEPT & PRODUCTION Ralf Hutter/Florian Schneider Klingklang Studio Dusseldorf, Russl Studio Hamburg

ARTISTE The Stranglers TITLE IV Rattus Norvegicus DATE 1977 COMPANY United Artists DESIGN Paul Henry
PHOTOGRAPHY Trevor Rogers

ARTISTE Fleetwood Mac TITLE Rumours DATE 1977 COMPANY Warner Bros DESIGN Deborah Strobel PHOTOGRAPHY Herbert Worthington CONCEPT Fleetwood Mac & Herbert Worthington

ARTISTE Ian Dury TITLE New Boots And Panties!! DATE 1977 COMPANY Stiff PHOTOGRAPHY Chris Gabrin

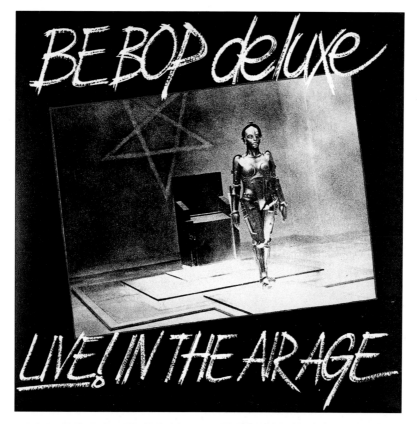

ARTISTE Be-Bop Deluxe TITLE Live! In The Air Age DATE 1977 COMPANY EMI
DESIGN Cream. Stills from Metropolis c/o Transit Filmgesell-Schaft GMBH

ARTISTE Greg Kihn TITLE Greg Kihn Again DATE 1977 COMPANY Beserkley PHOTOGRAPHY John Jensen

WIRE

ARTISTE Wire TITLE Pink Flag DATE 1977 COMPANY EMI DESIGN B.C. Gilbert & Lewis PHOTOGRAPHY Annette Green

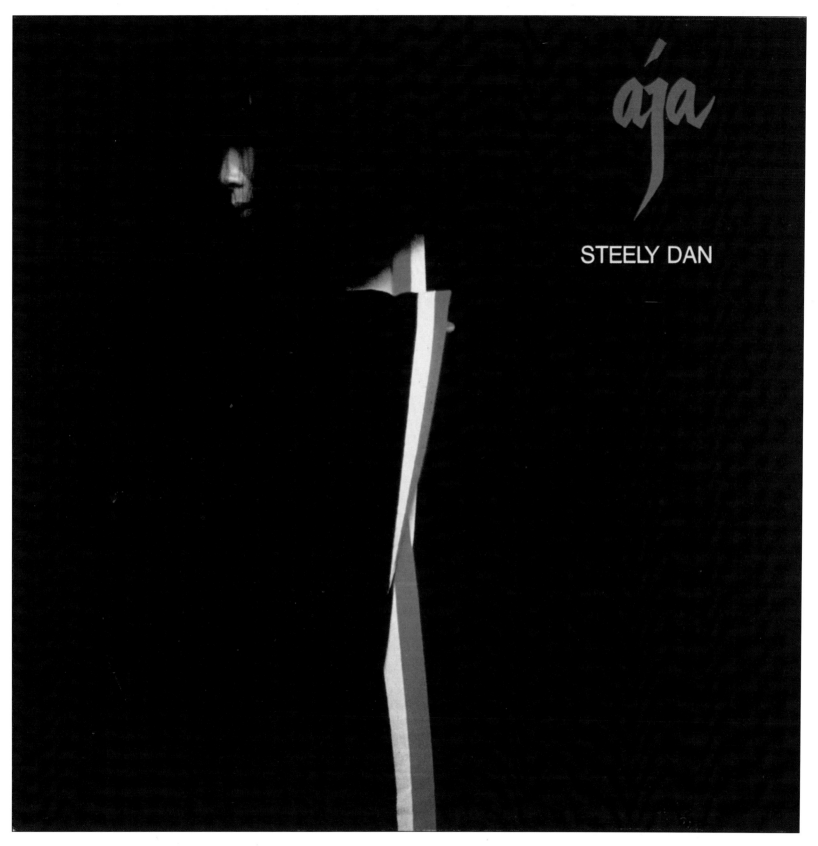

ARTISTE Steely Dan TITLE Aja DATE 1977 COMPANY ABC DESIGN Patricia Mitsui PHOTOGRAPHY Hideki Fujii ART DIRECTION OZ Studios

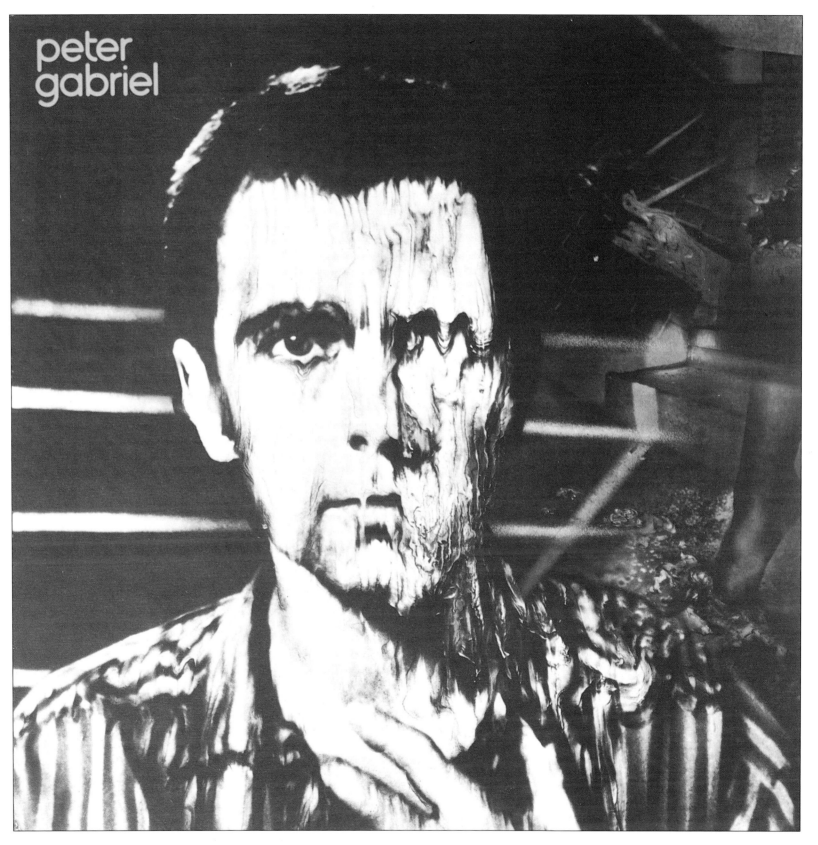

ARTISTE Peter Gabriel TITLE Peter Gabriel COMPANY Charisma DESIGN & PHOTOGRAPHY Hipgnosis

ARTISTE Meat Loaf TITLE Bat Out Of Hell DATE 1977 COMPANY Epic DESIGN Ed Lee ILLUSTRATION Richard Corben

ARTISTE The Boomtown Rats TITLE The Boomtown Rats DATE 1977 COMPANY Ensign DESIGN Geoff Halpin PHOTOGRAPHY Hannah Sharn ART DIRECTION Sue Dubois

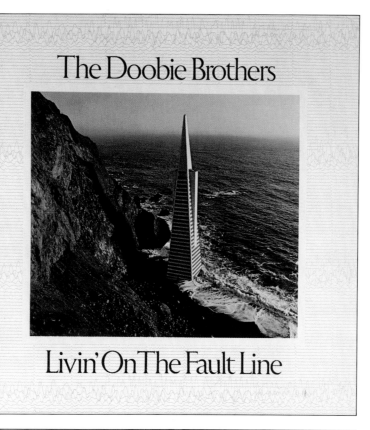

ARTISTE The Doobie Brothers TITLE Livin' On The Fault Line DATE 1977 COMPANY Warner Bros
DESIGN & PHOTOGRAPHY Bruce Steinberg

ARTISTE Weather Report TITLE Heavy Weather DATE 1977 COMPANY Columbia/CBS DESIGN Nancy Donald
ILLUSTRATION Lou Beach

ARTISTE Pink Floyd TITLE Animals DATE 1977 COMPANY EMI DESIGN Roger Waters PHOTOGRAPHY Hipgnosis/Howard Bartrop

PLAN FOR BLACKS TO WIN POWER IN RHODESIA

15 February The Rhodesian white leader Ian Smith and three black leaders, including Bishop Abel Muzorewa, announced a plan today to move the country to majority rule. Andrew Young, US Ambassador to the United Nations, said he believed it would lead to a blood bath.

OPPOSITION TO SHAH GROWING IN IRAN

11 May Screaming 'down with the Shah', thousands of demonstrators rioted in Tehran and other parts of Iran today, whipped up by religious leaders. The Shah cancelled a proposed trip to Hungary, claiming to 'have a cold', but it is obvious that the situation demands his presence in the country's capital. The Iranian government says the unrest 'will no longer be tolerated'.

ABUSING MPS UPSET RADIO LISTENERS

6 June Three days after the introduction of live transmissions of MPs at work, Parliament is at risk of becoming a laughing stock. William Price, the government minister responsible for the broadcasts, said he thought most people would be 'appalled by the bellowing, abuse, baying, hee-hawing and the rest'. He declared this afternoon: 'We have a public relations disaster on our hands. The nation cannot stand this shock!'

FIRST BABY BORN FROM TEST TUBE

26 July The world's first 'test-tube baby' was delivered at around mid-night last night, by Caesarean section, in Oldham District General Hospital. Mrs Lesley Brown, the mother, was said to be 'enjoying a well-earned sleep'. Dr Patrick Steptoe, who pioneered the technique, said that examinations showed the baby was quite normal. At any rate, the child's financial future seems safe, as newspaper rights to the story have been sold for £300,000.

NEW POPE DIES AFTER 33 DAYS IN OFFICE

30 September Pope John Paul was discovered at 5.30 a.m. today by his private secretary, apparently the victim of a heart attack. It is the shortest papal reign since Stephen II died two days after his election in 752.

MASS SUICIDE IN GUYANA

29 November In one of the largest ever mass suicides, nearly 1,000 members of a religious cult known as the People's Temple have been found dead in the verdant jungles of Guyana. Survivors claim their leader, the Rev. Jim Jones, who peopled the Jonestown commune with followers from his San Francisco mission, often rehearsed the cultists in acts of self-destruction, and finally convinced them to do it as 'an act of revolutionary suicide to protest at the conditions of an insane world'.

ARTISTE Generation X **TITLE** Generation X **DATE** 1978 **COMPANY** Chrysalis **DESIGN & PHOTOGRAPHY** Gered Mankowitz **TYPOGRAPHY** Geoff Halpin **ART DIRECTION** Peter Wagg

ARTISTE Vibrators TITLE Baby Baby COMPANY Epic (CBS) DESIGN Knox

ARTISTE The Adverts TITLE Safety In Numbers COMPANY Anchor DESIGN Nicholas De Ville

ARTISTE The Sex Pistols TITLE Holidays In The Sun COMPANY c/o Virgin DESIGN Jamie Reid

ARTISTE Damned TITLE Problem Child COMPANY Stiff DESIGN Barney Bubbles

ARTISTE Siouxsie and the Banshees TITLE The Scream DATE 1978 COMPANY Polydor DESIGN Jill Mumford PHOTOGRAPHY Paul Wakefield

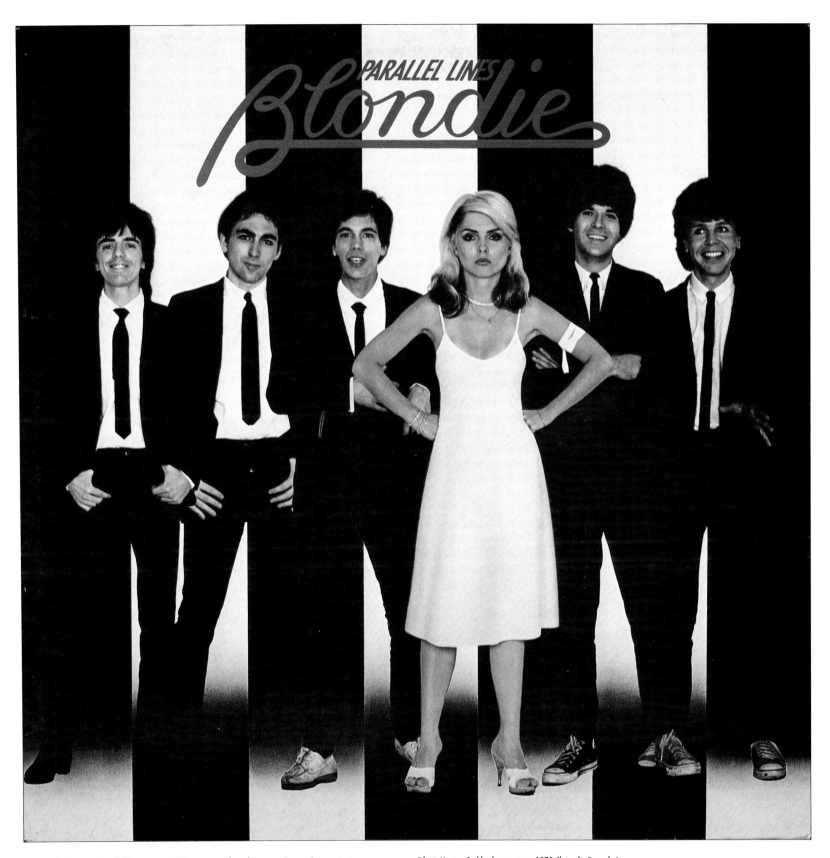

ARTISTE Blondie TITLE Parallel Lines DATE 1978 COMPANY Chrysalis DESIGN Ramey Communications PHOTOGRAPHY Edo & Martyn Goddard COPYRIGHT 1978 Chrysalis Records Inc

ARTISTE Joe Walsh TITLE But Seriously, Folks... DATE 1978 COMPANY Asylum DESIGN & PHOTOGRAPHY Jimmy Wachtel

ARTISTE Strawbs TITLE Deadlines DATE 1978 COMPANY Arista DESIGN Hipgnosis

ARTISTE Rolling Stones TITLE Some Girls DATE 1978 COMPANY Rolling Stones DESIGN CONCEPT Peter Corristan

ARTISTE Peter Gabriel **TITLE** Peter Gabriel **COMPANY** Charisma **DESIGN** Hipgnosis

ARTISTE Devo **TITLE** Q: Are We Not Men? **DATE** 1978 **COMPANY** Stiff **DESIGN** Devo
PHOTOGRAPHICS & LAYOUT Jeff Seibert **PHOTOGRAPHY** Greg Kaiser

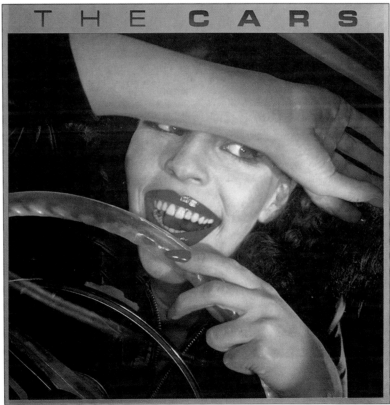

ARTISTE Squeeze TITLE Take Me, I'm Yours DATE 1978 COMPANY A & M
DESIGN Nick Marshall ART DIRECTION Michael Ross PHOTOGRAPHY George Greenwood

ARTISTE The Cars TITLE The Cars DATE 1978 COMPANY Elektra/Asylum DESIGN Johnny Lee
ART DIRECTION Ron Coro

ARTISTE Be-Bop Deluxe TITLE Drastic Plastic DATE 1978 COMPANY Harvest (EMI) DESIGN & PHOTOGRAPHY Hipgnosis

ARTISTE Kate Bush TITLE The Kick Inside DATE 1978 COMPANY EMI DESIGN Splash Studios PHOTOGRAPHY Jay Myrdal CONCEPT Kate Bush

ARTISTE Kraftwerk TITLE The Man Machine DATE 1978 COMPANY Capitol PHOTOGRAPHY Gunter Frohling

PUBLIC IMAGE

first issue

public image
THEME
Annalisa

ARTISTE Public Image Limited TITLE Public Image DATE 1978 COMPANY Virgin DESIGN Zebulon CONCEPT Terry Jones & Dennis Morris

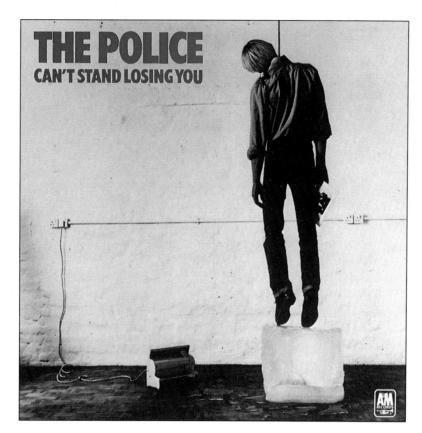

ARTISTE The Police **TITLE** Can't Stand Losing You **DATE** 1978 **COMPANY** A & M **DESIGN** Michael Ross
PHOTOGRAPHY Peter Gravelle

ARTISTE Patti Smith **TITLE** Because The Night **DATE** 1978 **COMPANY** Arista

ARTISTE Magazine TITLE Real Life DATE 1978 COMPANY Virgin DESIGN Linder

THATCHER WINS ELECTION

4 May With the election of Britain's first ever woman prime minister, the Tories rule Britain again. At 10 Downing Street a triumphant 53-year-old Margaret Thatcher quoted from St Francis of Assisi this afternoon: 'Where there is discord may we bring harmony... Where there is despair may we bring hope.'

ENGLISH SOCCER FANS RIOT IN STREETS.

12 June Italian police fired tear gas during England's opening match of the European championship in an attempt to break up rioting British supporters. About a hundred youths charged at Belgian supporters when their team equalized. Play had to be stopped to allow players to recover from the effects of the gas.

BREZHNEV AND CARTER SIGN SALT TREATY

18 June The leaders of the world's two superpowers, Jimmy Carter and Leonid Brezhnev, today signed the SALT-2 arms limitation treaty in Vienna's Hofburg Palace. 'We are helping to defend the most sacred right of every man. The right to live,'said Mr Brezhnev, who later seemed on the point of collapse.

ECONOMISTS CLAIM RECESSION ON THE WAY

1 July Job losses are reaching 40,000 a month as industry braces for what is predicted to be the worst depression since World War II. Economists feel that unemployment will pass the two million mark by next summer. Union bosses slammed the government today, claiming its monetary policy is weakening the country's industrial base.

JOE JACKSON

LOOK SHARP!

ARTISTE Joe Jackson TITLE Look Sharp! DATE 1979 COMPANY A & M DESIGN Michael Ross PHOTOGRAPHY Brian Griffin

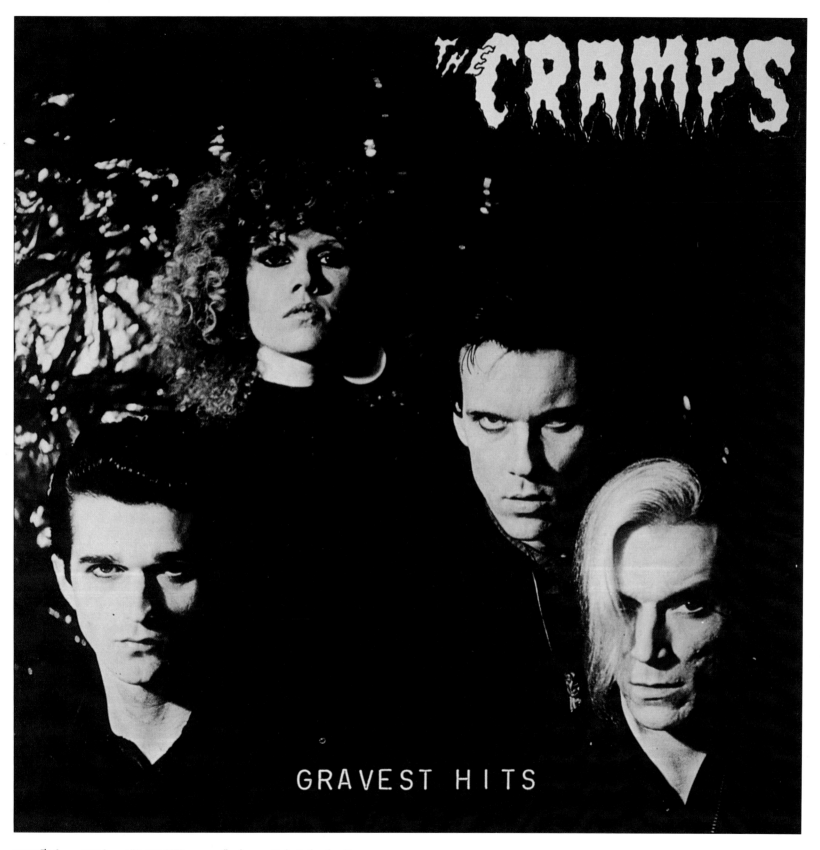

THE CRAMPS

GRAVEST HITS

ARTISTE The Cramps TITLE Gravest Hits DATE 1979 COMPANY Illegal DESIGN Stephanie Chernikowski

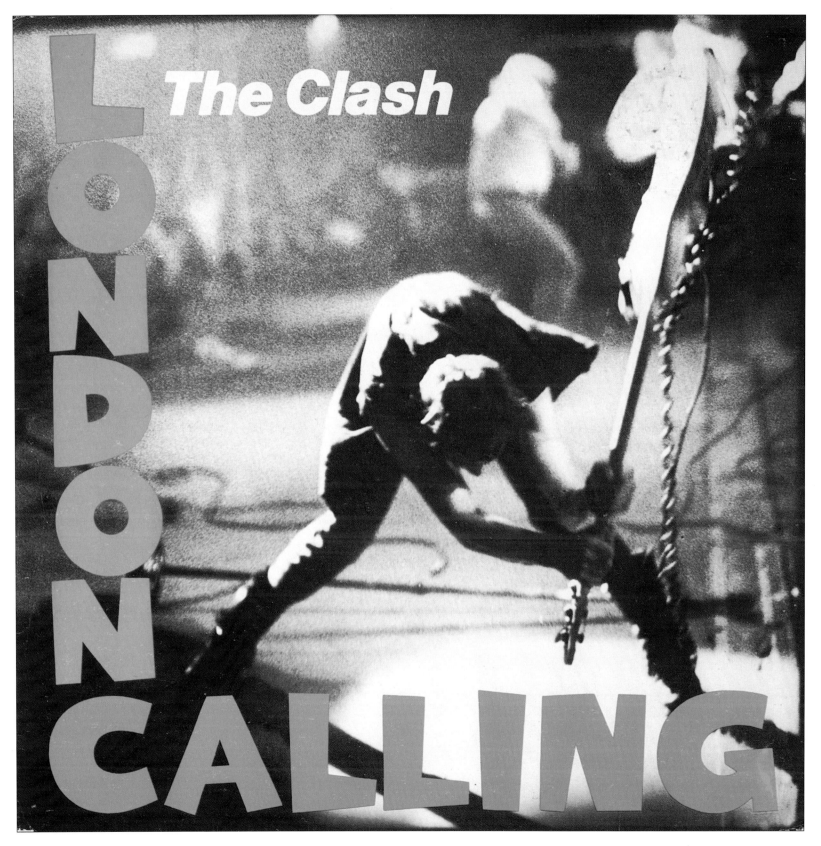

ARTISTE The Clash TITLE London Calling DATE 1979 COMPANY CBS DESIGN Ray Lowry PHOTOGRAPHY Pennie Smith

ARTISTE The Slits TITLE Cut DATE 1979 COMPANY Island PHOTOGRAPHY Pennie Smith DESIGN Bloomfield/Travis

ARTISTE The Pop Group TITLE Y DATE 1979 COMPANY Warner Bros DESIGN Donald McCullin & Ian Denning

ARTISTE Robert Palmer **TITLE** Secrets **DATE** 1979 **COMPANY** Island **DESIGN & PHOTOGRAPHY** Graham Hughes

ARTISTE The Motels TITLE The Motels DATE 1979 COMPANY Capitol DESIGN Roy Kohara/Henry Marquez PHOTOGRAPHY Elliot Gilbert NEON John Uomoto

ARTISTE Buzzcocks TITLE A Different Kind Of Tension DATE 1979 COMPANY Liberty DESIGN Malcolm Garret & Accompanying Images PHOTOGRAPHY Jill Furmanovsky

ARTISTE David Bowie **TITLE** Lodger **DATE** 1979 **COMPANY** RCA **DESIGN** Duffy

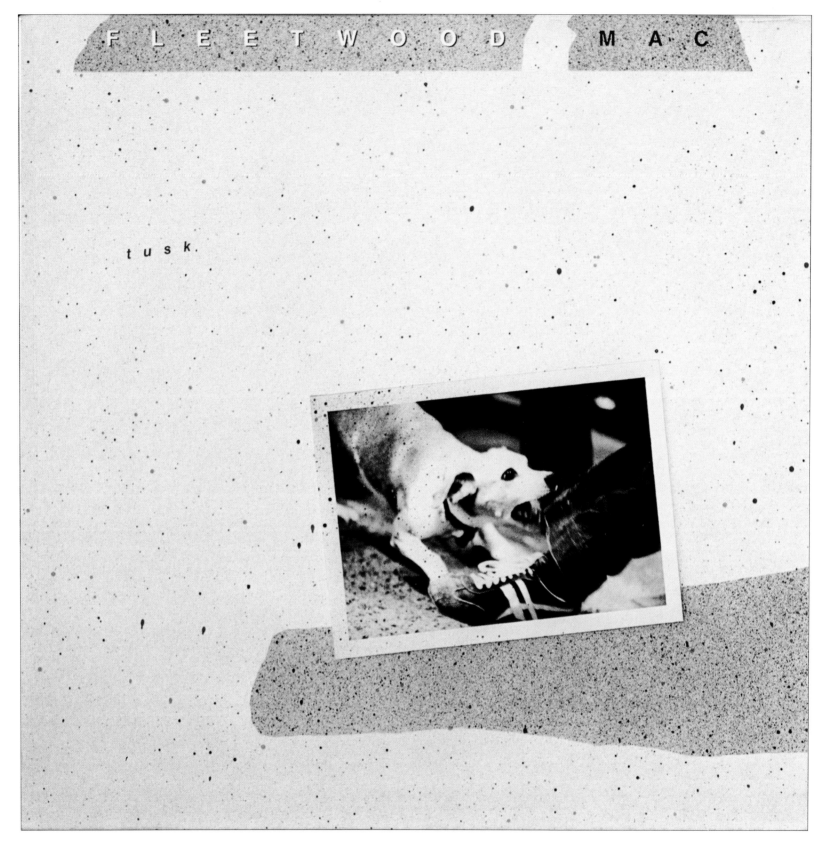

FLEETWOOD MAC

tusk

ARTISTE Fleetwood Mac **TITLE** Tusk **DATE** 1979 **COMPANY** WEA **DESIGN & ART DIRECTION** Vigon Nahas Vigon **PHOTOGRAPHY** Peter Beard/Jayme Odgers/Norman Seeff

171

the quality of mercy is not strnen

The MEKONS

ARTISTE The Mekons TITLE The Quality Of Mercy Is Not Strnen DATE 1979 COMPANY Virgin DESIGN The Mekons/Cooke Key PHOTOGRAPHY Brian Cooke

ARTISTE The Tubes **TITLE** Remote Control **DATE** 1979 **COMPANY** A & M **DESIGN** Michael Cotton/Prairie Prince **PHOTOGRAPHY** Jim McCrary **ART DIRECTION** Roland Young **CO-ORDINATION** Chuck Beeson & Jeff Ayeroff

THAT SUMMER!

IAN DURY   ELVIS COSTELLO   THE PATTI SMITH GROUP

THE BOOMTOWN RATS

NICK LOWE

ZONES

RICHARD HELL

THE UNDERTONES

WRECKLESS ERIC

THE RAMONES

MINK De VILLE   EDDIE & THE HOT RODS   THE ONLY ONES

ARTISTE Various TITLE That Summer! DATE 1979 COMPANY Arista DESIGN Graphyx

174

ARTISTE Sham 69 TITLE The Adventures Of Hersham Boys DATE 1979 COMPANY Polydor DESIGN Jo Mirowski PHOTOGRAPHY Peter Lavery

ARTISTE XTC TITLE Drums And Wires DATE 1979 COMPANY Virgin DESIGN Andy Partridge ILLUSTRATION Jill Mumford

ARTISTE Simple Minds TITLE Life In A Day DATE 1979 COMPANY Zoom DESIGN & PHOTOGRAPHY Carole Moss Type Graphyk

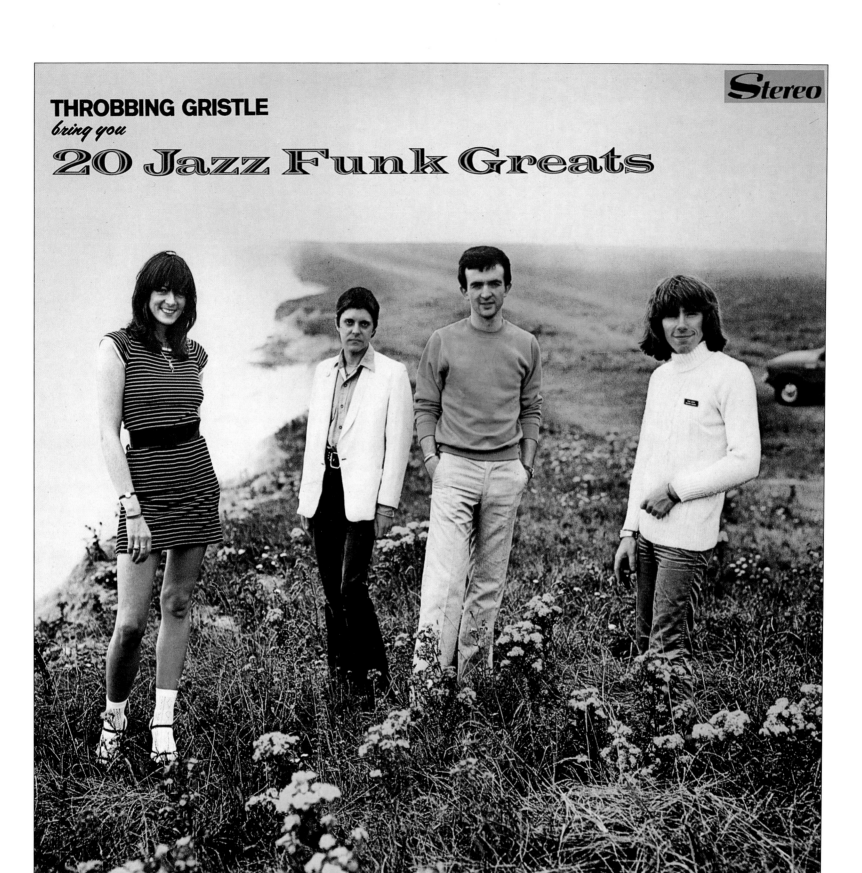

ARTISTE Throbbing Gristle TITLE 20 Jazz Funk Greats DATE 1979 COMPANY Industrial DESIGN Peter Christopherson

ARTISTE Public Image Limited TITLE Metal Box DATE 1979 COMPANY Virgin DESIGN CONCEPT John Lydon ART DIRECTOR Charles Dimont

ARTISTE Yellow Magic Orchestra TITLE Yellow Magic Orchestra DATE 1979 COMPANY A & M DESIGN Amy Nogasawa & Chuck Beeson ILLUSTRATION Lou Beach

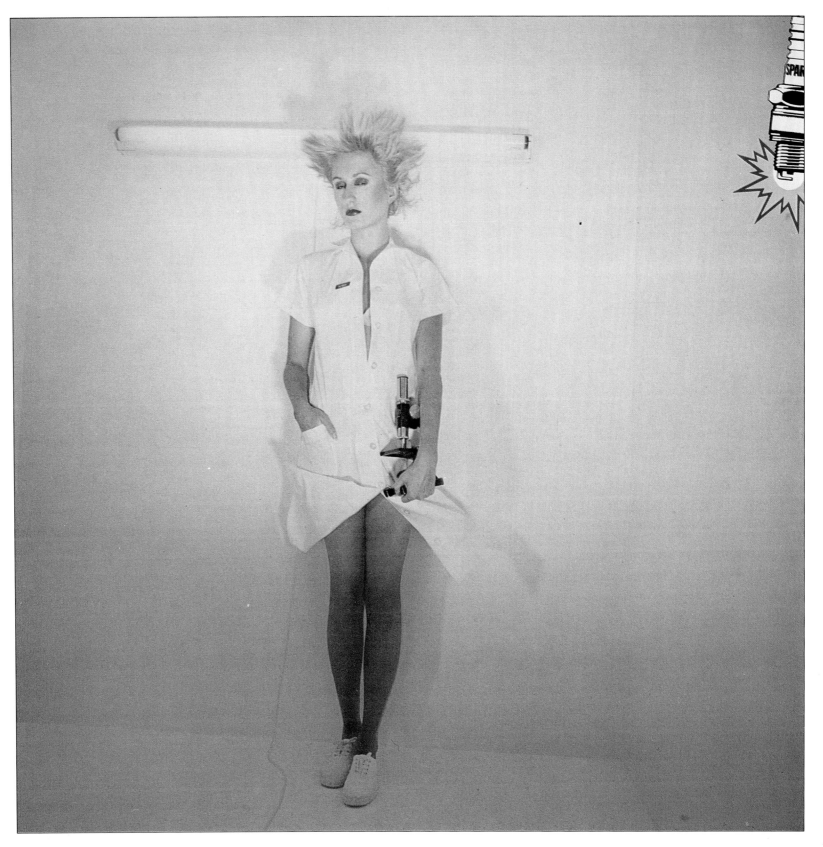

ARTISTE Sparks TITLE No. 1 In Heaven DATE 1979 COMPANY Virgin

ARTISTE Jefferson Starship TITLE Freedom At Point Zero DATE 1979 COMPANY Grunt DESIGN Lewerke-Shapiro PHOTOGRAPHY Gary Regester STAR SCOUT Tyrone Q. Thompson

ARTISTE Flash And The Pan TITLE Flash And The Pan DATE 1979 COMPANY Epic DESIGN Janet Perr & Gene Greif PHOTOGRAPHY Ken Ambrose

ARTISTE Streetband TITLE Dilemma DATE 1979 COMPANY Logo DESIGN Bill Smith PHOTOGRAPHY Bishin Jumonji (Courtesy of the Mitsubish Electric Industry Co. Ltd)

ARTISTE Madness TITLE One Step Beyond DATE 1979 COMPANY Stiff DESIGN Eddie & Jules PHOTOGRAPHY Cameron McVey

ARTISTE Scorpions TITLE Lovedrive DATE 1979 COMPANY Harvest DESIGN & PHOTOGRAPHY Hipgnosis

economic climate. Why bother with the expense of going to Egypt with a 10" x 8" camera and crew when a tatty Polaroid shot backstage after a club gig would do? It was a healthy and necessary change, inevitable and essential. The pendulum was moving swiftly across the grandfather clock and, as my grandfather would have said, 'pack up' before they pack you up.

A new wave of cover designers came on the scene, such as Neville Brody, Peter Saville and Malcolm Garratt. All out of the late seventies, they stormed the eighties and are still along for the ride in the nineties. But the small CD is here, and so is the even smaller DAT, and the four decades of vinyl are over. Enjoy the indulgent graphics of the seventies, as this particular format is unlikely to be repeated.

Aubrey Powell, 1994

Biography

AUBREY 'PO' POWELL founded the now highly acclaimed design company Hipgnosis with Storm Thorgerson in 1968 after graduating from the London School of Film Technique. Album cover designs undertaken include work for Led Zeppelin, Paul McCartney, Pink Floyd, Bad Company, Genesis, Yes, Peter Gabriel and 10cc to name but a few. In 1982 Po, Storm and Peter Christopherson formed Green Back Films, making music videos for artists such as Paul Young, Robert Plant and Yes. In 1985 Aubrey began Aubrey Powell Productions in partnership with Peter, expanding into television commercials, documentaries and feature films.

Aubrey Powell's most recent work includes directing the movie *Cure Show* for The Cure and the high definition Fuji television presentation of Paul McCartney's *Soundcheck*. He also directed Paul McCartney's television documentary *Moving On* in 1993 which was nominated for the Golden Rose of Montreux award.

He is obsessed with long-distance sailing, travels constantly, and continues to be active in film, music and literature. Although based in London, his leisure time is spent with his children in either Bequia or Ibiza.

Index

Album titles are shown in italic

IV Rattus Norvegicus 133
10cc
   How Dare You 114
   Sheet Music 38
20 Jazz Funk Greats 178
999
   Nasty Nasty 130

A Different Kind Of Tension 169
A Wizard 65
Adverts, The
   Safety In Numbers 146
After the Goldrush 47
Agharta 104
Aja 138
Aladdin Sane 67
All Aboard 126
American Beauty 27
Animals 143
Another Green World 111
Atlantic Crossing 113
Atom Heart Mother 11
Audience
   Lunch 51
Axe Victim 87

Baby Baby 146
Bark 26
*Baron von Tollbooth And The
   Chrome Nun* 57
Barrett, Syd
   The Madcap Laughs 14
Bat Out of Hell 140
Be-Bop Deluxe
   Axe Victim 87
   Sunburst Finish 123
   Live! In The Air Age 136
   Drastic Plastic 154
Beach Boys, The
   Surf's Up 35
Because The Night 158
Billion Dollar Babies 62
Bitches Brew 21

Black Sabbath
   Never Say Die! 121
Bley, Paul
   Copenhagen And Haarlem 104
Blondie
   Parallel Lines 149
Blue Oyster Cult
   Secret Treaties 76
Blues For Allah 99
Boomtown Rats, The 141
Borboletta 82
Bowie, David
   Ziggy Stardust 41
   Aladdin Sane 67
   Diamond Dogs 79
   Heroes 131
   Lodger 170
Brain Salad Surgery 37
Brand X
   Unorthodox Behaviour 124
Breakfast In America 187
Browne, Jackson
   Late For The Sky 71
Buckley, Tim
   Greetings From L.A. 45
Bush, Kate
   The Kick Inside 155
But Seriously, Folks.... 150
Buzzcocks, The
   A Different Kind Of Tension 169
Byrds, The
   Sweetheart of the Rodeo 18

Cactus Choir 125
Cale, John
   Vintage Violence 33
   Fear 88
Can I Have My Money Back? 30
Can't Stand Losing You 158
Candy-O 165
Captain Beefheart
   The Spotlight Kid 46
   Trout Mask Replica 109
Caravanserai 49
Cars, The
   The Cars 153

Candy-O 165
Catch A Fire 63
Clash, The
   The Clash 132
   London Calling 163
Close To The Edge 44
Cochise 16
Cooder, Ry
   Ry Cooder 17
   Into The Purple Valley 25
Cooper, Alice
   School's Out 42
   Billion Dollar Babies 62
   Muscle of Love 66
   *Welcome To My
   Nightmare* 108
Copenhagen And Haarlem 104
Country Life 80
Cramps, The
   Gravest Hits 162
Crime Of The Century 78
Crosby, Stills, Nash & Young
   Deja Vu 50

Daltrey, Roger
   Ride A Rock Horse 107
Damned, The
   Problem Child 147
Dark Side Of The Moon 55
Davis, Miles
   Bitches Brew 21
   Agharta 104
Dawn Hearts 32
Deadlines 150
Deep End 115
Deep Purple
   Stormbringer 77
Deja Vu 50
Devo
   Q: Are We Not Men? 152
Diamond Dogs 79
Dilemma 184
Do You Wonder 107
Doobies Brothers, The
   Livin' On The Fault Line 142
Doors, The

Morrison Hotel 19
   Full Circle 56
Down On The Farm 166
Dragonfly 92
Drastic Plastic 154
Dressed To Kill 110
Drums and Wires 176
Dury, Ian
   New Boots and Panties!! 135

Eddie And The Hot Rods
   Teenage Depression 127
Electric Light Orchestra
   Face The Music 102
Elegy 29
Emerson, Lake & Palmer
   Brain Salad Surgery 37
Eno
   Another Green World 111
Exile On Main Street 43

Face The Music 102
Faces, The
   Ooh La La 58
Fear 88
Flash And The Pan 183
Fleetwood Mac
   Heroes Are Hard To Find 90
   Fleetwood Mac 110
   Rumours 134
   Tusk 171
For Your Pleasure 40
Force It 111
Freedom at Point Zero 182
Full Circle 56
Fumble 50

Gabriel, Peter 139, 152
Garcia, Jerry 88
Generation X 145
Genesis
   Nursery Cryme 28
   *The Lamb Lies Down On
   Broadway* 74

Giels, J.
   Ladies Invited 66
God Save The Queen 132
Grateful Dead
   Workingman's Dead 20
   American Beauty '2/
   Blues For Allah 99
Gravest Hits 162
Greenslade, Dave
   Cactus Choir 125
Greetings From Asbury
   Park N.J. 69
Greetings From L.A. 45
Greg Kihn Again 136

Hagen, Nina
   Unbehagen 165

Hard Nose The Highway 64
Harris, Eddie
   Is It In 86
Hasten Down The Wind 106
Havens, Ritchie
   The End of The Beginning 119
Hawkwind
   In Search of Space 31
Heavy Weather 142
Heroes 131
Heroes Are Hard To Find 90
Holidays In The Sun 147
Houses Of The Holy 61
How Dare You 114
Humble Pie
   Smokin' 39

Iggy & The Stooges
   Raw Power 67
Illusion 87
In Search Of Space 31
In The City 130
Indelibly Stamped 83
Indiscreet 97
Into the Purple Valley 25
Is It In 86
Isotope
   Illusion 87
   Deep End 115

J. Giels Band, The
   Ladies Invited 66

Jackson, Joe
   Look Sharp! 161
Jam
   In The City 130
James Montgomery
   Band, The 118
Jefferson Airplane
   Bark 26
Jefferson Starship
   Dragonfly 92
   Freedom at Point Zero 182
Jethro Tull
   Thick As A Brick 51
Journey 112
Jump On It 124

Kantner, Paul
   see Paul Kantner
Kihn, Greg
   Greg Kihn Again 136
Kiss
   Kiss 72
   Dressed To Kill 110
Kraftwerk
   The Man Machine 156
   Trans Europe Express 133

Ladies Invited 66
Late For The Sky 71
Led Zeppelin
   Houses Of The Holy 61
   Led Zeppelin III 15
   Led Zeppelin IV 24
   Physical Graffiti 103
   Presence 117
Life In A Day 177
Little Feat
   Down On The Farm 166
Live at Leeds 15
Live! In The Air Age 136
Livin' On The Fault Line 142
Lodger 170
London Calling 163
London Symphony Orchestra
   Tommy 48
Look Sharp! 161
Lovedrive 186
Lunch 51

Mad Shadows 12
Made In The Shade 73

Madness
   One Step Beyond 185
Magazine
   Real Life 159
Manfred Mann's Earth Band
   The Roaring Silence 123
Meat Loaf
   Bat Out Of Hell 40
Mekons, The
   The Quality Of Mercy Is Not
   Strnen 172
Metal Box 179
Miller, Steve
   The Joker 53
Mitchell, Joni
   The Hissing Of Summer
   Lawns 122
Montgomery, James 118
Montrose
   Jump On It 124
Morrison Hotel 19
Morrison, Van
   Hard Nose The Highway 64
Motels, The 168
Mothers Of Invention, The
   Weasels Ripped My Flesh 13
Mott The Hoople
   Mad Shadows 12
   The Hoople 89
Muscle Of Love 66
Mustard 95
Mysterious Traveller 93

Nasty Nasty 130
Never Mind The Bollocks Here's
   The Sex Pistols 129
Never Say Die! 121
New Boots And Panties!! 135
Nice, The
   Elegy 29
Nina Hagen Band
   Unbehagen 165
No. 1 In Heaven 181
Nursery Cryme 28
Nutz 72

Oldfield, Mike
   Tubular Bells 54
On The Beach 91
On The Frontier 59
One Step Beyond 185

Ooh La La 58
Osibisa 30

Palmer, Robert
   Sneakin' Sally Through
   The Alley 81
   Secrets 167
Parallel Lines 149

Paul Kantner, Grace Slick and
   David Freiburg
   Baron Von Tollbooth And The
   Chrome Nun 57
Peter Gabriel 139, 152
Phenomenon 90
Phillips, Shawn
   Do You Wonder 107
Physical Graffiti 103
Pink Flag 137

Pink Floyd
   Atom Heart Mother 11
   Dark Side of The Moon 55
   Wish You Were Here 101
   Animals 143
Playing Possum 106
Police, The
   Can't Stand Losing
   You 158
Pop Group, The
   Y 164
Presence 117
Pretty Things, The
   Silk Torpedo 75
Problem Child 147
Public Image Limited
   Public Image 157
   Metal Box 179

Q: Are We Not Men? 152

Rafferty, Gerry
   Can I Have My Money
   Back? 30
Ramones 126
Raw Power 67
Real Life 159
Relayer 84
Remote Control 173
Ride A Rock Horse 107

Rolling Stones, The
  Sticky Fingers 23
  Exile On Main Street 43
  Made In The Shade 73
  Some Girls 151
Rondstadt, Linda
  Hasten Down The Wind 106
Roogalator
  All Aboard 126
Roxy Music
  For Your Pleasure 40
  Stranded 60
  Country Life 80
Rumours 134
Rundgren, Todd
  A Wizard 65
Ry Cooder 17

Safety In Numbers 146
Santana
  Santana 34
  Caravanserai 49
  Borboletta 82
  Greatest Hits 94
Scaggs, Boz
  Silk Degrees 120
School's Out 42
Scorpions
  Lovedrive 186
Secret Treaties 76
Secrets 167
Seventh Wave
  Things To Come 85
Sex Pistols, The
  Never Mind The Bollocks 129
  God Save The Queen 132
  Holidays In The Sun 147
Sham 69
  The Adventures Of Hersham
    Boys 175
Sheet Music 38
Shoot
  On The Frontier 59
Silk Degrees 120
Silk Torpedo 75
Simon, Carly
  Playing Possum 106
Simple Minds
  Life In A Day 177
Siouxsie And The Banshees
  The Scream 148
Slits, The 164

Smith, Patti
  Because The Night 158
Smokin' 39
Sneakin' Sally Through
  The Alley 81
Some Girls 151
Sparks
  Indiscreet 97
  No. 1 In Heaven 181
Springsteen, Bruce
  Greetings From Asbury Park N.J.
    69
Squeeze
  Take Me, I'm Yours 153
Steely Dan
  Aja 138
Steve Miller Band, The
  The Joker 53
Stevens, Cat
  Teaser And The Firecat 31
Stewart, Rod
  Atlantic Crossing 113
Sticky Fingers 23
Stormbringer 77
Stranded 60
Stranglers, The
  IV Rattus Norvegicus 133
Strawbs, The
  Deadlines 150
Streetband
  Dilemma 184
Sunburst Finish 123
Supertramp
  Crime Of The Century 78
  Indelibly Stamped 83
  Breakfast In America 187
Surf's Up 35
Sweetheart of the Rodeo 18

Take Me, I'm Yours 153
Tales From Topographic
  Oceans 68
Teaser And The Firecat 31
Ted Nugent's Amboy Dukes
  Tooth, Fang & Claw 73
Teenage Depression 127
That Summer! 174
The Adventures Of Hersham
  Boys 175
The Edgar Winter Band with Rick
  Derringer 100
The End of The Beginning 119

The Hissing Of Summer
  Lawns 122
The Hoople 89
The James Montgomery Band 118
The Joker 53
The Kick Inside 155
The Lamb Lies Down On
  Broadway 74
The Low Spark Of High Heeled
  Boys 24
The Madcap Laughs 14
The Man Machine 156
The Quality of Mercy is Not
  Strnen 172
The Roaring Silence 123
The Scream 148
The Spotlight Kid 46
Thick As A Brick 51
Things To Come 85
Throbbing Gristle
  20 Jazz Funk Greats 178
Time And A Word 14
Tommy 48
Tooth, Fang & Claw 73
Traffic
  The Low Spark Of High Heeled
    Boys 24
Trans Europe Express 133
Trout Mask Replica 109
Tubes, The
  The Tubes 86
  Remote Control 173
Tubular Bells 54
Tusk 171

Unbehagen 165
UFO
  Phenomenon 90
  Force It 111
Unorthodox Behaviour 124

Van Der Graaf Generator
  Dawn Hearts 32
Venus And Mars 105
Vibrators
  Baby Baby 146
Vintage Violence 33

Wailers, The
  Catch A Fire 63

Walsh, Joe
  But, Seriously Folks.... 150
Weasels Ripped My Flesh 13
Weather Report
  Mysterious Traveller 93
  Heavy Weather 142
Welcome To My Nightmare 108
Who, The
  Live At Leeds 15
Wings
  Venus And Mars 105
Winkies, The 179
Winter, Edgar 100
Wire
  Pink Flag 137
Wish You Were Here 101
Wood, Roy
  Mustard 95
Workingman's Dead 20

XTC
  Drums and Wires 176

Y 164
Yellow Magic Orchestra 180
Yes
  Time And A Word 14
  Close To The Edge 44
  Tales From Topographic
    Oceans 68
  Relayer 84
Young, Neil
  After The Goldrush 47
  On The Beach 91

Ziggy Stardust 41